INSIGHT COMPACT GUIDE

Men

Compact Guide: Menorca is the ultimate quick-reference guide to this popular destination. It tells you everything you need to know about Menorca's attractions, from its wide choice of bays and beaches to its fascinating prehistoric monuments, from the streets and squares of Ciutadella to the villages and hills of the interior.

This is one of 133 Insight Compact Guides, which combine the interests and enthusiasms of two of the world's best-known information providers: Insight Guides, whose titles have set the standard for visual travel guides since 1970, and Discovery Channel, the world's premier source of nonfiction television programming.

APA PUBLICATIONS
Part of the Langenscheidt Publishing Group

Insight Compact Guide: Menorca

Written by: Thomas Gebhardt
English version by: Paul Fletcher
Photography by: Bill Wassman
Additional photography by: Gordon Singer (pages 9, 35, 92, 101, 102)
Cover picture by: Greg Evans
Design: Vicky Pacey
Picture Editor: Hilary Genin
Maps: Polyglott/Buchhaupt
Design concept: Carlotta Junger

Editorial Director: Brian Bell
Managing Editor: Tony Halliday

● **CONTACTING THE EDITORS:** As every effort is made to provide accurate information in this publication, we would appreciate it if readers would call our attention to any errors and omissions by contacting:
Apa Publications, PO Box 7910, London SE1 1WE, England.
Fax: (44 20) 7403 0290
e-mail: insight@apaguide.demon.co.uk

Information has been obtained from sources believed to be reliable, but its accuracy and completeness, and the opinions based thereon, are not guaranteed.

© 2003 APA Publications GmbH & Co. Verlag KG Singapore Branch, Singapore.

First Edition 2002; Updated 2003
Printed in Singapore by Insight Print Services (Pte) Ltd
Original edition © Polyglott-Verlag Dr Bolte KG, Munich

Worldwide distribution enquiries:
APA Publications GmbH & Co. Verlag KG (Singapore Branch)
38 Joo Koon Road, Singapore 628990
Tel: (65) 6865-1600, Fax: (65) 6861-6438

Distributed in the UK & Ireland by:
GeoCenter International Ltd
The Viables Centre, Harrow Way, Basingstoke,
Hampshire RG22 4BJ
Tel: (44 1256) 817987, Fax: (44 1256) 817-988

Distributed in the United States by:
Langenscheidt Publishers, Inc.
46–35 54th Road, Maspeth, NY 11378
Tel: (1 718) 784-0055, Fax: (1 718) 784-0640

www.insightguides.com

Menorca

Introduction

Places

Culture

Travel Tips

◁ **Albufera d'es Grau (p62)** The second-largest wet biotope in the Balearics, this important nature reserve attracts a wealth of birdlife.

▽ **Fornells (p66)** This oasis on the north coast is famous for its spiny lobster dish, *caldareta de langosta*.

▽ **Santa Maria, Maó (p27)** As well as a busy port, the island's capital has many fine buildings. Here in the main church you can hear organ recitals in the summer.

▽ **Naveta d'es Tudons (p60)** This Bronze Age burial chamber is the most famous prehistoric monument in Menorca. It is thought to be the oldest roofed building in Europe.

△ **Alaior (p53)** Built on a hilltop, with narrow streets, colourful houses, decorated balconies and fine courtyards, Alaior stands out as one of the prettiest towns in Menorca. It is also the principal manufacturer of the island's most famous cheese, *Queso de Mahón*.

△ Son Catlar (p88)
This prehistoric village is one of the finest in all the Balearic Islands. Inhabited until the fall of the Roman Empire, it is now a UNESCO site.

△ Cala en Turqueta (p87) Menorca is famous for its beaches — it has one for each day of the year. Some are crowded, others remote and only accessible on foot. This shallow bay with its fine sandy beach is ideal for families with children.

◁ Binibeca Vell (p73)
Built in direct contrast to the high-rise hotels, this resort has won prizes for its original architecture.

◁ Ciutadella (p35)
With its narrow alleyways, Gothic churches, sunny squares and a beautiful harbour, Ciutadella has much to offer the visitor.

▷ Monte Toro (p56)
On the top of Menorca's highest peak stands a massive statue of Christ.

The Green and Blue Island

Opposite: sailing around Illa d'es Llatzaret
Below: cycling by Son Saura
Bottom: relaxing on Playa Ferragut

As far as tourism is concerned, Menorca has always been the low-key destination among the Balearics. It is much more intimate and subtle than Mallorca, with its grandiose scenery, and does not have the raucous nightlife of Ibiza. There once seemed to be no seductive attributes, until the island gradually started to discover itself – and realised that its own, largely intact, natural environment was actually something very special. Elsewhere, tourists are attracted – or repelled – by all the hustle and bustle; the unspectacular, modest little island of Menorca, however, provides them with a magic that makes it appear a real oasis.

Menorca wasn't discovered by the tourist industry until relatively late, and escaped the worst excesses of the 1960s and 1970s. Now a series of strict environmental regulations have prevented people from trying to catch up on what they thought they missed. A lot of beaches really are unspoilt; prehistoric sites have been spared snack bars and souvenir stands; and the towns have grown naturally. Tourist enclaves there undoubtedly are, but in comparison to Ibiza and Mallorca, Menorca is a peaceful, laid-back haven, its resorts ideal for family holidays.

It is also the only one of the Balearic Islands to have been declared a biosphere reserve by UNESCO – a decision that has made its neighbours exceedingly envious. The island known as the Isla Verde y Azul (Green and Blue Island) has finally discovered itself.

LOCATION

Whenever the sun rises in Spain it always rises first above Menorca, the easternmost and also northernmost of the Balearic Islands, which lies on 4° longitude and 40° latitude. This means that Sardinia, the Iberian peninsula, Marseilles and Algiers are all roughly equidistant from it. On a clear day, Mallorca is visible from the Cap

CLIMATE CHART

Mahón

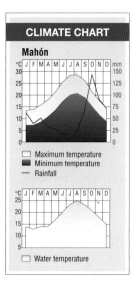

☐ Maximum temperature
■ Minimum temperature
— Rainfall

☐ Water temperature

A lazy day near Son Saura

d'Artrutx, the southwestern point of Menorca, and is only 20 nautical miles distant – the equivalent of 37km (23 miles).

From a distance Menorca may not look all that special, but close up the island's unique charm unfolds. The 285km (177 miles) of coastline encircle an island that is far more varied than could ever be imagined from the tourist brochures: despite its relatively small size it has enchanting bays, fantastic beaches and extremely varied landscapes.

CLIMATE AND WHEN TO GO

The Mediterranean climate gives Menorca hot, humid summers and mild, frequently rainy winters. Basically those are the only two seasons on the island. Visitors who come here in the peak travel season (June, July or August) usually come for sunshine and the seaside, and generally only need luggage for the beach, town visits and evening entertainment, plus sturdy shoes for the odd hike. Daytime temperatures of 30°C (86°F) and over are no rarity, and the water temperature is always above 20°C (68°F).

If you can manage it, try to come to Menorca off-season. The daytime temperatures are moderate, the sea is still reasonably warm, the beaches are deserted and the silent megalithic settlements and muted colours make the island a very special experience in the months of April, May and September. Hikers and culture seekers will be relieved to discover that the island's interior, far from the beaches, is not as oppressively hot either during these months.

At the end of October, when hotels and holiday resorts close down all over the island, the first rain showers arrive, heralding the start of the Menorcan winter. Around 80 percent of the annual precipitation falls between now and March. Between December and February the island is also exposed now and then to the *tramuntana*, a cold north wind from the Pyrenees. The temperatures don't actually drop below zero at these times, but the weather is certainly a lot less pleasant. Menorca is less suitable for a winter visit than its larger neighbour. If you decide to go anyway, then take waterproofs and plenty of warm clothing.

LANDSCAPE

Put somewhat over-simply, Menorca has two main regions: the Tramuntana in the north and the Migjorn in the south. The Tramuntana is distictive for its steep and high coastline, bizarre rock formations and fjord-like inlets. There is not very much vegetation, apart from the forested area of La Vall near the Patjes d'Algaiarens. Slate-like, reddish-black stone tends to predominate.

Below: digging at Cala Santa Galdana
Bottom: Fornells harbour

Limestone karst regions are the most significant feature of the south of the island, which is gentler despite its lack of trees and vegetation. The coastline is flatter than the north, and this is where the much-praised bays and beaches are to be found. A total of 36 drainage valleys known as *barrancs* have cut their way through the Migjorn; they are biotopes, shielded from the wind, and also green oases for fertile fields or for almost impenetrable plant cover. The geological dividing line between the north and south runs roughly from the capital Maó in the southeast to Cala Morell in the northwest.

Rivers or streams on Menorca very rarely have water in them the whole year round; the only one

Well-forested nature reserve

that does, in fact, is the Torrent d'Algendar; otherwise there are just a few small streams. The Albufera d'es Grau in the east of the island, however, is the second-largest marshland biotope in the Balearic Islands.

The centre of Menorca is full of fertile fields and meadows, pine groves and the odd forest of cork oak, and there is also a low range of hills which appear more like a central mountain range because the island is otherwise so flat. The highest points on the island – the Monte Toro (357m/1,70ft), Enclusa (275m/900ft) and the Puig de Santa Àgueda (264m/866ft) – certainly give travellers an overview, however.

DRYSTONE WALLS

Surveying Menorca from the top of Monte Toro, the island looks like a large patchwork quilt, divided up by a labyrinth of drystone walls known as *parets seques*. The walls partition fields, surround farms and follow lanes and tracks all the way to the outskirts of Maó and Ciutadella. Depending on the time of year, the resulting landscape can be reminiscent of lush green Devon or sun-baked Malta.

Skilfully constructed, the walls taper in towards the top; and most of them are around twice the height of walls on the other Balearic islands. They are more extensive too, covering a total length of some 15,000km (9,400 miles).

OLD PATHS ON MENORCA

These days, accustomed to short routes, we forget how difficult travelling used to be. Crossing the island from west to east, for instance, took at least two and a half days until the 18th century. The terrain was difficult, and sections of an almost 2000-year-old Roman road were used. Carts had to be loaded and unloaded so they and their contents could be heaved across ravines, because the Camí Real, or Royal Way, built after the *Reconquista*, wasn't all that royal after all and only existed in sections.

All this changed when Menorca's first British governor, Sir Richard Kane (1660–1736), arrived. His practical nature turned out to be a blessing: he introduced new types of fruit and the Friesian breed of cattle, and financed water cisterns for entire villages out of his own pocket. Most important of all he commissioned the construction of the first proper connecting road between east and west, the **Camí d'en Kane.** It's well worth getting to know the 16km (10 miles) or so that still survive of this route *(see page 50).*

THE HORSES' WAY

The **Camí de Cavalls**, or Horses' Way, is the name of a coastal path that was originally constructed for military horseback patrols back in the Middle Ages. A ring road around the island seems impossible today because the deep ravines known as *barrancs* could not be crossed without bridges, but in the old days dispatch riders had to make their way from one watchtower to the next to warn of enemy attacks.

In the 18th century, during the seven-year French occupation, the horses' trail was repaired in places and continued to be used by the Spanish army until the 1960s, before being abandoned. Subsequently, the island council declared several stretches to be 'objects of public interest', and

Below: Camí way marker
Bottom: parets seques

since then various sections of the Camí de Cav-alls have been renovated, notably from Cala Pre-gonda in the north past Cala Pilar to Cala en Carbó, and in the south from Cala Santa Gal-dana to Cala en Turqueta. It will be a while, how-ever, before pedestrians and horses will be able to walk or ride round the whole island.

FLORA

Even though large areas of Menorca look green, the vegetation is actually less profuse than on the other Balearic Islands. The *tramuntana* wind prevents some plants that flourish on Mallorca from growing here at all. There are few citrus or almond trees, but plenty of olive trees and oleast-ers, which can brave any wind.

Below: spring meadow
Bottom: traditional May dance

Gnarled, windswept oleasters can often even be seen clinging to the steep cliffs. Their hard wood is used by the locals to make the numer-ous gates that often have to be opened and closed during hikes across the island.

There are no extensive forested areas, but pines and evergreen oaks cover almost 30 percent of Menorca. Mastic trees, the resin from which is used for glue, and chest-high macchia – wide-spread in the Mediterranean – cover the whole island with their colours and aromas, as does a local variety of flowering yellow gorse.

Up to 200 different plant species can grow in a single *barranc* here, and some of them are real botanical rarities, often only found on the Balearic Islands, such as some subspecies of carob and peony. Pomegranate trees and bushes grow primarily in the south of the island and are harvested in the autumn, together with figs and wine.

Coming to Menorca in the springtime is a memorable experience: the place is a flower-filled paradise. The meadows and roadsides are covered with foxgloves, crocuses and wild orchids.

FAUNA

Even though there are several reptiles and rodents here – numerous lizards, non-poisonous grass snakes, short-legged Balearic voles and also a near-extinct species of wild rabbit – Menorca is primarily remarkable for its bird-life. There are redthroats, blackthroats, nightingales, hoopoes, turtle doves and ring doves, to name but a few.

In the marshland areas of S'Albufera d'es Grau and Es Prat de Son Bou there are moorhen, waterfowl and grey herons; nearby or along the rocky coast, kites and buzzards have their nests, and there's even a species of vulture native to the island.

To gain an impression of the aquatic life around the island the best thing to do is examine the menus outside the seafood restaurants – there's still a huge variety, even though the waters here are considered over-fished.

PEOPLE

The 65,000 or so Menorcans are fiercely proud of their island and the quality of life it provides. They're also hospitable and sociable, and it's easy to get involved in conversation – in a cafe, at a *branca* game (the Spanish version of *boules*) or at one of the numerous festivals that take place at different times of the year. Don't worry if your Catalan or Spanish isn't up to it – the important thing is human communication.

The Menorcans have a reputation for being self-confident – this may, however, have partly

Ornithologists
Ornithologists should read the book *Birds of Menorca*, published by the GOB *(Grup Ornitológic Balear)* and available in English, German, Catalan and Castilian.

Below: rugged karst scenery
Bottom: a Ciutadella woman

👁️ **English influence**
Dominated by the British for most of the 18th century, it is not surprising that an enduring colonial legacy lives on in Menorca – in the architecture, the customs, and, most intriguingly, in the local dialect. Menorquí is peppered with Anglicisms at every level, from the most superficial to the most profound. Some, like *vermell com un Jan* (red like an Englishman) and *ball des cosil* (Scottish dances), are colloquialisms that have worked their way in; others are direct Menorquinisations of English words. For example, *tornescru* and *bech* are the islanders' versions of the words 'screwdriver' and 'back' – totally unconnected to their Spanish equivalents of *destornillador* and *respaldo*.

originated from the need to look good in the face of their big sister Mallorca just across the water.

A historic rivalry still exists between the people of Maó and those of Ciutadella, the towns in which two-thirds of the island's population live. The British deprived Ciutadella of its capital city status in the 18th century and granted it to Maó, a reason why the latter's inhabitants are still teasingly called *ingléses* (Englishmen) now and then. Their response to this is to refer to everyone outside the capital as provincials – to the great annoyance of the people of Ciutadella, in particular.

Much of this is in good humour, however, and there are plenty of things that bind the two together: a deep religious faith (churches are still very well attended), opulent festivals for their patron saints, and last but not least, *Menorquí*, their common language.

MENORQUI – THE ISLAND'S LANGUAGE

The roots of *Menorquí*, one of the oldest versions of *Catalá* (Catalan), go back a long way. When Menorca was conquered by Alfonso III in 1287 and was settled by Catalonian farmers and craftsmen, *Catalá* – an important language in medieval times, and of Latin origin – arrived on the Balearic Islands. The union of Catalonia and Castile raised Castilian to the level of official national language,

Everyday discourse, Ciutadella market

but the Spanish still speak a variety of regional languages, and *Catalá* is one of them. It was suppressed several times over the centuries – including during Franco's dictatorship, which lasted until his death in 1975 – and was not allowed to be taught or printed. Things changed a lot after Franco died, however.

Menorquí, which still contains elements of Arabic, French and English, and stayed reasonably separate from Catalan over the centuries, now has a new lease of life. Eighty percent of lessons in the island's schools are in *Menorquí*; Catalan has been the official language of the Balearic Islands since the late 1970s, but islanders all speak Spanish as well. Place-name signs have been rewritten and some villages actually renamed, which can sometimes be confusing for tourists.

Map publishers are often unable to keep up with the latest changes, and some still take you to San Cristóbal instead of Es Migjorn Gran; the names of pubs and inns frequently retain the old names as well. The capital of the island took a long time to replace the name Mahón with the Catalan name Maó, but that change, too, has now been made (all the place names in this guide are in Catalan). If you do get lost, try a cheerful *On és..?* (Catalan for 'where is?') or *Donde està..?* (the Castilian equivalent) and you should be able to reach your destination without a problem.

Local produce ranges from gin to cheese.

ECONOMY

Claims about Menorca not being dependent on tourism because of its flourishing fish, agriculture, jewellery and leather goods industries have not been true for a long time now. The formerly important fishing fleet has dwindled to 150 boats, which only just cover the island's needs.

The situation facing agriculture is similar: just 6 percent of the workforce is employed in it. Dairy farming and horse-breeding tend to predominate. Cheese production (5,000 tons a year) is still important, and Queso de Mahón is still a well-known brand name beyond the island's borders – but it accounts for just 320 dairy farming jobs and

Jewellery

In the early part of the 20th century the harbours of Menorca shipped fashion jewellery to Europe and America. British officers' wives very much appreciated the brooches and silver-studded handbags, and Menorcan jewellery was soon a regular sight in the world's fashion shops. In those days a workforce of around 3,000 processed 15,000kg of silver annually to keep up with demand. All that is now history, of course. Not much remains of the once-flourishing trade, though the fine work of the island's coppersmiths and silversmiths in Alaior and Ciutadella is still an integral part of the SEBINE fashion jewellery fair, held in May every year.

Checking departure times

a few dozen cheese producers. Spain's entry into the European Union in 1986 also imposed quota limitations: cattle numbers had to be reduced by around one third to 25,000.

The traditional footwear and leather goods industry manufactures products for Italian and French companies, and also supplies other European countries with brands such as Pons Quintana and Gomila, but is relatively small.

The jewellery industry is having to combat cheap imports from the Far East or competitive products from Portugal and the Spanish mainland, and production has long since been limited to a handful of manufacturers or cottage businesses.

TOURISM

Economic diversity has been enhanced by Menorca's status as a UNESCO biosphere reserve, with the aim of sustaining tourism development within the framework of conservation and support for local industry. Even so, Menorca has not been immune from the islands' tourism explosion. In 1950, the island had just 200 hotel beds; now there are 40,000 and almost a million visitors a year. Apart from the 18 percent of the population who work in banking, 56 percent of Menorcans live directly or indirectly from tourism: waiters, hotel owners, windsurfing instructors, sales people. This is one reason why so much fuss was made when the 25 millionth air passenger arrived on the island back in 1995.

More than half the holidaymakers come from the UK, followed by those from Germany, Spain and Italy. Since the beach and suntan season is limited to the period between May and September, 24 percent of Menorcans are unemployed during the winter months. The money and tips earned during the holiday season often has to tide tourism workers over into the next one.

POLITICS AND ADMINISTRATION

When Franco died in 1975, Spain was radically reorganised: the country received a democratic constitution and was transformed into a parliamentary democracy, with centralism replaced by pluralism. Under a Statute of Autonomy in 1978 the Balearic Islands were one of 17 regions to be given a measure of autonomy. In 1983, they officially became Comunidad Autónoma de las Islas Baleares, with Palma de Mallorca as their capital. There the *Govern Balear* – the provincial government – has a reasonable amount of say in the islands' affairs, especially in matters concerning culture, education, tourism, energy management and construction.

Each island also has its own *Consell Insular*, or island council, which is an organ of the government and the executive, and has powers ranging from the control of archaeological investigations on prehistoric sites to issues regarding tourism, construction and social policy.

Communal matters are taken care of by the mayors and municipal councils of the eight Menorcan administrative districts.

In elections, Menorca tends to vote less conservatively than the other Balearic Islands. The winners of the last regional elections in June 1996, however, were not the PSOE (Socialists) but the Conservative PP (Partido Popular). The latter's narrow majority was due to its support for tourist expansion, which many Menorcans regard as a never-ending source of money.

Below: local and EU flags
Bottom: a crowded Cala Santa Galdana

HISTORICAL HIGHLIGHTS

ca 5000BC First signs of settlement on Menorca by gatherers and fishermen from southern France and eastern Spain who constructed large cave complexes.

From 2000BC Walled settlements and stone structures are built by the megalithic Talayot culture: they leave fortified towers *(talayots)*, table-shaped cult sites *(taulas)*, and burial chambers *(navetes)*, shaped like upturned boats.

ca 1000BC Phoenicians begin trading with the island, which they call Nura (Island of Fire), probably deriving from warning fires along the coast. The settlements of Mogona (Mahón) and Iamnona (Ciutadella) date from this time.

ca 400BC The Balearic Islands are taken over by the Carthaginians. The countryside is exploited for agriculture; oil and wine are the principal products.

205BC Carthage falls to Rome after the Punic wars. Romans annex the Balearics.

123BC Mallorca and Menorca occupied by the Romans. Menorca receives the name Balearis Minor.

AD200 Balearics convert to Christianity.

426 Vandals devastate the islands, and persecute the Christians. Trade declines.

534–902 Vandals defeated by Byzantines; Christianity restored; the Balearics become part of the Byzantine Empire.

902 The islands conquered by the caliphs of Cordoba. Around 1000, Medina Minurka (Ciutadella) is made the capital. The Balearics remain under Moorish rule until the 13th century, and flourish culturally. Menorca becomes a fortified base for Mediterranean pirates.

1015 The collapse of the caliphate of Cordoba; the Balearics annexed to the small Muslim kingdom of Denia.

1087–1114 The islands become an independent kingdom, which is known as the *taifa* of Mallorca.

1203–29 The Balearics fall into the hands of Almohadian tribes from Algeria and Denia. Resulting political instability lays the islands open to foreign occupation.

1229 Jaume I of Aragon occupies Mallorca; he conquers Menorca in 1232.

1276 Death of Jaume I; the kingdom is divided. Menorca becomes part of the newly created Kingdom of Mallorca.

1287 Reconquest of Menorca by Alfonso III of Aragon and Catalonia.

1298 Alfonso's successor, Jaume II of Aragon, returns the Kingdom of Mallorca (including Menorca) to his exiled uncle, Jaume II of Mallorca.

1312–24 The reign of Jaume III brings great economic prosperity to the islands.

1344 Troops of Pedro IV of Aragon invade and reincorporate the Balearics into the Kingdom of Aragon. Immigrants from Catalonia arrive, bringing their language with them; the towns of Alaior, Es Mercadal and Ferreries are founded.

1349 Jaume III tries to recover the Kingdom of Mallorca but dies in battle.

1469 Marriage between Isabela of Castile and Ferdinand of Aragon unites the Spanish crowns: the Catholic Monarchs rule all of Spain, including the Balearics, from 1479.

16th century The island is attacked on numerous occasions by Ottoman and Moorish fleets. Spanish king, Charles V, has fortresses built to protect the towns.

1558 Following a 10-day siege, Ciutadella is almost completely destroyed by a 15,000-strong Turkish army.

1708 Menorca is seized by the British during the War of the Spanish Succession – a move that is sanctioned by the 1713 Treaty of Utrecht.

1722 The British shift the capital from Ciutadella to Mahón (Maó).

1756–63 French troops occupy the island and found the town of Sant Lluís. Under the Treaty of Paris, Menorca is handed back to Britain.

From 1763 Numerous fortifications are built, including the Georgetown garrison, later to become Villa Carlos and then Es Castell.

1781–2 Franco-Spanish troops land on Menorca, and the island falls to Spain. All fortifications removed. Economic decline sets in.

1795 The diocese of Menorca is established, with Ciutadella as its bishopric.

1802 The Treaty of Amiens gives the island to Spain once and for all.

1803–13 The War of Independence against Napoleon. Refugees arrive, provoking social and political unrest.

First half of the 19th century Numerous Menorcans emigrate to Northern Africa, especially Algeria.

1879–98 Period of social and commercial success ends when the phylloxera virus destroys the wine industry. Economic decline results in widespread emigration to the mainland and to the USA.

1936 Franco leads uprising against Spain's Republican government. Mallorca and Ibiza support Franco's Nationalists but Menorca backs Republicans in the ensuing Spanish Civil War. The island falls to Franco's troops in 1939.

1939–45 Spain plays no part in World War II.

1953 The first charter plane lands on Menorca and the age of tourism begins.

1975 On Franco's death, Spain becomes a constitutional monarchy under King Juan Carlos I.

From 1978 Spain gets a democratic constitution. The Balearics become one of 17 autonomous regions, with Palma de Mallorca as the capital. Menorca's Island Council is formed in 1979.

1986 Spain joins the European Community (later the European Union).

1991 The Balearic parliament passes an environmental protection act; one-third of Menorca turned into a nature reserve.

1993 UNESCO declares Menorca a biosphere reserve.

1997 Cultural Tourism Plan bears fruit, with an increase in reconstruction work on cultural monuments all over Menorca.

1989–2001 The economy prospers; the Balearics enjoy the highest per capita income in Spain. Continuing renaissance in literature and arts. Steps taken to limit the damage inflicted by mass tourism and take the industry upmarket.

2002 The euro becomes the currency of Spain.

Map on page 24

1: Maó

Maó is a city that has always attracted admiring comments. A glowing travel account by Roy W. Baker, the American consul in Barcelona, appeared in the *National Geographic Magazine* in 1928. He described the Menorcan capital as 'a maze of blinking alleyways leading up and down hill, lined with bright dolls' houses'. Maó, located at the end of a long, narrow bay, was at that time one of the finest harbours in the Mediterranean. Baker also mentioned that the place had the feel of an English provincial town, and that still applies today.

A VERY BRITISH TOWN

Preceding page: Ciutadella by night
Below: Maó street sign
Bottom: Maó harbour

At first sight this little city, with a population of 21,600, seems more restrained than one would expect in these latitudes. This is probably because it had rulers of several different nationalities in the past, due to its strategic location. The British, who held Menorca throughout the 18th-century and made Maó the island's capital, introduced several very English elements: sash windows, green shutters and brass door knockers among them. There's even a gin distillery. The two main churches were also built during the years of British rule. In many ways, however, everything

is very Spanish, as you will find if you go to the market in the Claustre del Carme, for example *(see page 30)*.

HISTORY

If the legend is true, Maó owes its existence to Mago, the brother of Hannibal, who visited the island to recruit Menorcan slingers – experts at fighting with the slingshot – in around 205BC. Etymologically it is more likely, however, that the name derives from the Phoenician word *maghen*, meaning 'fortification'.

After the Phoenicians and Carthaginians, it was the turn of the Romans to marvel at the harbour's perfect strategic location. In the 1st century AD they made Magona into Portus Magonis, and it soon became an important harbour town. The Romans also built a road to *Iamnona*, today's Ciutadella. The Romans were followed by the Byzantines, and then the Moors, who were driven from Menorca in 1287 by Alfonso III of Aragón.

The 16th century brought renewed attacks by Moorish and Ottoman pirates, and Maó lost many of its inhabitants as a result. Charles V had a further wall built to protect the harbour entrance. On their next visit to the island the Turks decided to move on to Ciutadella, which they duly razed to the ground *(see page 35)*.

CHANGES IN GOVERNMENT

In 1708, during the War of the Spanish Secession, the British occupied Menorca, and in 1722 they elevated Maó to the status of island capital. Under Sir Richard Kane, the first British governor, a well-surfaced road was built from the city to Ciutadella. The harbour was extended, and new fortifications such as Fort Marlborough were built. British influence is visible everywhere in Maó today, especially in the architecture; the French were only here for eight years and little of their influence remains.

In 1802, after Menorca had fallen to Spain once and for all under the terms of the Treaty of Amiens,

Strategic location
Maó has always been at the centre of the island's turbulent history. Its long, deep harbour has provided protection for the city's rulers, but also borne the brunt of numerous invasions. The result is a city whose influence is greater than its size.

Traditional transport in the Plaça de la Constitució

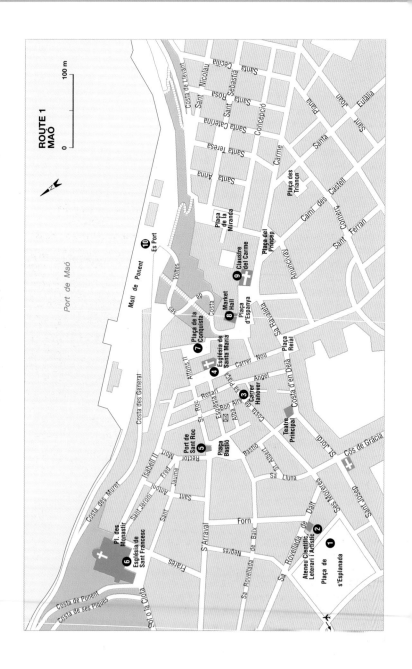

ROUTE 1
MAÓ

0   100 m

Port de Maó

Moll de Ponent

Es Port

Costa de Levant

Sant Nicolau   Santa Cecília

Sant Rosa   Santa Sebastià

Santa Caterina   Concepció

Santa Teresa   Carme

Santa Anna

Plana   Sant Joan   Eulàlia

Santa

Castell

Camí des

Plaça des Trianon

Sant Comerç

Sant Ferran

Plaça del Príncep

Plaça de la Miranda

Claustre del Carme ⑨

Market Hall ⑧

Plaça d'Espanya

Sa Ravaleta

Anuncivài

Costa

ses

Portes

Alfons II

Plaça de la Conquista ⑦

Església de Santa Maria ④

Carrer Nou

Plaça Reial

Rosari

Sant Roc

Església des Alba

Bon Aire

Plaça des Alba

Costa d'en Deià

Carrer Hanover ③

Angel

Teatre Principal

Costa des General

Port de Sant Roc ⑤

Plaça Bastió

Rector

Mort

Bastió

Sant Albert

Sa Lluna

Sant Isabel

St. Jordi

Cos de Gràcia

Isabell II

Frau

Sant Jaume

Sant Antoni

Sant Jeroni

Costa des Muret

Forn

Sant

Pl. des Monastir

Església de Sant Francesc ⑥

S'Arraval

de Baix

Negres

Sa Rovellada de Dalt

Ses Moreres

Sant Roc

Ateneu Científic Leterari i Artístic ②

Plaça de s'Esplanada ①

Frares

Sa Rovellada de Baix

Costa de Ponent

Costa de ses Piques

Con la Clota

the once-popular metropolis was forgotten for several decades. Today, however, Maó is the economic heart of Menorca and still the capital. The new Spanish constitution of 1978 gave autonomy to 17 regions and five years later the islands officially become the Comunidad Autónoma de las Islas Baleares. Since then Menorca's fortunes have been steered to a large extent from Palma de Mallorca. The *Consell Insular* in Maó only has responsibility for archaeological, agricultural, constructional and social issues.

SIGHTS

The large **Plaça de s'Esplanada ❶** was formerly used by the British as a parade ground. Most of the important access streets end here, and an underground car park swallows up visitors' cars. The rectangular, palm-lined square is a good place to observe Menorcan life at any time of day. A market is held here onTuesday and Saturday, drawing visitors in from the surrounding resorts.

Every day, from early morning, you can see old people sitting in cafés such as the Cafeteria Consey or on stone benches beside hibiscus bushes, chatting together or reading the latest edition of *Menorca – Diario Insular*. Children clamber up climbing frames, while soldiers guard the formerly British-owned barracks. An obelisk commemorates those who fell in the Spanish Civil War (1936–39). If you are looking for information, go to the tourist office just off the eastern side of the square in Carrer Sa Rovellada de Dalt.

Below: crossing the Plaça Esplanada
Bottom: altarpiece, Maó

CULTURAL CENTRE

Opposite the tourist office is the **Ateneu Cientific, Leterari i Artístic ❷** (Mon–Fri 10am–2pm, 4–10pm, Sat 10am–2pm), an old-fashioned place that is home to Menorca's most important cultural association. It contains a library with a reading room and numerous tomes on the island's history, a collection of landscapes and still-lifes, ceramic plates and wall tiles. You will have to ask if you want to see the antechamber full of stuffed

Map on page 24

Organ recitals
Try to go to an organ recital in Santa Maria if you get the chance. In the summer months there are recitals every day but Sunday at 11am, and international organists perform during the evening. CDs are also on sale as souvenirs .

native birds, fish in formalin, seashells and minerals that are kept under lock and key.

The shopping street Carrer de des Morreres is very busy all year round and souvenir, fashion and food shops vie for the custom of local people and tourists. A bust commemorates Dr Mateo José Orfila (1787–1853) who was born at No. 13 and went on to found modern toxicology and pathology in the distant Institut Pasteur in Paris. He also invented a method of tracing arsenic.

In the narrow alleyway of Costa D'en Deià you will suddenly find yourself confronted by the **Teatre Principal**. The Italian architect and tenor Giovanni Palagi designed the original building and the curtain first rose here in 1829, before that of the Teatro Real in Madrid. Very little today remains of the glorious days of opera, when Italian ensembles began their tours of Spain in Maó. The theatre has recently been given a complete make-over and there is a full progamme of performances, but very few operatic ones these days.

CARRER HANOVER

A decorated Plaça Colom

Back to the busy shopping street, which then becomes the steep ★ **Carrer Hanover** ❸. The name is a reminder of the connections between the English royal family and the House of Hanover, and also of a Hanoverian regiment formerly stationed at the Plaça d'Esplanada.

This street is extremely tempting for a shopping expedition, but its architectural style should not be overlooked as it is very English and typical of Maó. There are sash windows on every house and door handles that need to be pushed downwards – the Menorcans call them *pestells*. The bow windows are known as *boinders*, and a particularly ornate one can be seen at the corner of Carrer Bastio.

On the little Plaça Colom, with its statue of a flower girl – framed by four palm trees, four benches and four basins – is a bookshop with an interesting selection of Balearic and Menorcan literature, plus a music shop selling popular *cantantes nacionales*.

SANTA MARIA

The Plaça de La Constitució is dominated by the ★★**Església de Santa Maria** ❹ (daily 7.30am–1pm and 6–8.30pm), which was built above the remains of an older structure between 1748 and 1772, in honour of the patron saint of Maó. The neo-classical façade is relatively unpretentious, while the single-aisled interior contains a variety of styles, ranging from a Gothic nave to rococo flourishes around the altar.

The most important object is the mighty organ, a masterpiece of its kind. In 1809 a Maó merchant commissioned the renowned Swiss organmaker Johann Kyburz to construct it, and a year later it arrived on the small Mediterranean island, complete with its four manuals and 3,006 organpipes. The instrument became famous for its uncannily realistic *vox humana*, and after extension and renovation work it now has 3,210 pipes, 215 of which are wooden.

THE TOWN HALL

The other fine building in this square is the **Ajuntament** (Town Hall), built on what was originally the site of the medieval fortress of Maó; only a few remains of foundation walls in the cellar survive from the earlier structure. The façade is crowned by a bell wall and clock tower, which

Star Attraction
• Església de Santa Maria

Below: the Santa Maria organ
Bottom: ceiling, Santa Maria

Map on page 24

Below: Town Hall entrance
Bottom: Arc de St Roc

was donated to the city by the first British governor, Sir Richard Kane *(see page 11)*. The interior of the Town Hall is British in style too: alongside portraits of Spanish governors and a Roman signet stone showing that Portus Magonis received civic rights in the 1st century AD, there is a portrait of the English king George III (1738–1820). The figures outside the main council chamber wearing Menorcan folk dress are almost 3m (10ft) high, and are carried through the streets of Maó during festive processions.

PORT DE SANT ROC

As you walk down the Carrer de Sant Roc, the late 15th-century ★ **Port de Sant Roc** ❺ will be seen ahead of you. This is the only one of Maó's mighty medieval town gates to have survived from the former fortifications and is now a national monument. It once marked the start of the long and arduous route to Ciutadella, and was also the town boundary until the 18th century. In a niche above it, enclosed in scruffy plexiglass, is a sculpture of St Roche, who is believed to have saved Maó from a plague outbreak.

A few steps lead up to the adjacent **Plaça del Bastió**, where restaurants and awnings provide a welcome rest. The *tapas variadas* are really good here and children will enjoy the rocking-horses and climbing equipment in the middle of the square.

TOWARDS THE MONASTERY

The Carrer des Rector Mort leads into what used to be the smartest suburb of Maó, which began spreading beyond the old town walls back in the 17th century. Just next to the narrowest building in the capital, the Carrer Fred branches off. No shop windows or advertisements break up the brownish-yellow façades here, although more than a touch of colour is added by washing on the lines stretched across the street. Old people sit and chat in the shade outside their front doors.

On the Plaça d'es Monestir is the ★ **Església de Sant Francesc** ❻ (daily 10am–noon, 5–7pm, except Thurs pm), built in 1791–92 as the church of a Franciscan monastery. Above the entrance doorway is a baroque *Annunciación*, and All Saints' Chapel inside illustrates the churrigueresque-baroque style with highly ornamental decoration, which is quite rare on this island.

The former monastery houses the extensive historical and archaeological collections of the ★★ **Museu de Menorca** (Tues–Sat 10am–2pm, 6–9pm, Sun 10am–2am). The highlights of which include *talayotic* finds as well as a Gothic stone with a Catalan inscription in memory of the *reconquista* of Menorca by Alfonso III.

PLAÇA DE LA CONQUISTA

Follow the Carrer d'Isabell II, and you will see the white, colonial-style palace of the former British governor, today the seat of the island's military administration, and several other smart-looking *palazzi*. One of the finest, at No. 42, is the headquarters of the biggest nature conservation society in the Balearic Islands. You will also pass a wonderful candle shop, the Cereria Abella.

Finally you'll be back at the Església de Santa Maria once more. The nave of the church separates the Plaça de la Constitució from the **Plaça**

Star Attraction
•Museu de Menorca

Harbour view
From the peaceful square in front of Sant Francesc there's a fantastic panoramic view of the harbour, and not far away the narrow alley called Costa d'es General leads down to the waterside. There is also an atmospheric shop on the square, selling pulses, rice and flour from huge sacks and with baskets hanging from the ceiling.

Sant Francesc

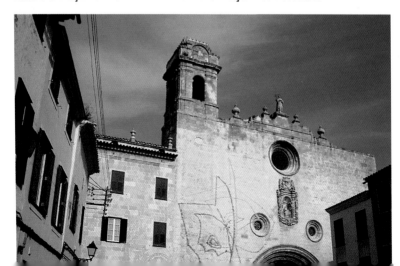

Map on page 24

Important collection
The Carmelite monastery houses the **Hernandez Mora Collection**, once the property of historian and philologist Dr Hernandez Mora, with historic engravings of the Mediterranean region, paintings, old maps, numerous items of furniture and also a library (Mon–Sat 10am–1pm).

Below: Alfonso III monument
Bottom: market stall

de la Conquista ❼, and the building dominates both squares. The patrician house Ca'n Mercadal contains the municipal library and in the centre of the square is a monument to Alfonso III. At the end of the small cul-de-sac called Pont d'es Castell – the name is a reminder of the drawbridge that was once located here – there is another fantastic view across the harbour.

MARKETS AND CLOISTERS

Anything the fishermen catch in their baskets and nets is up for sale at the ornate ★ **Mercat ❽** on the Plaça d'Espanya. Pike, flounder and stickleback lie on ice, and crustaceans – *mariscos* – are piled high. If you not only look but buy, you'll usually get a free handful of fresh parsley, as is the custom in Mediterranean countries.

Next door stands the neo-classical **Església del Carme** with its adjoining cloister, the **Claustre del Carme ❾**. The largest church in Maó, it was built between 1726 and 1808, and at that time it lay outside the city walls. Today it serves as a useful landmark for tour guides who want to reassemble their groups after shopping expeditions in the streets of Carrer Nou and Carrer Hanover, so the square in front of the church is often busy. The altar inside has some interesting medallions depicting the life of the Virgin Mary.

The Carmelite monastery served as a judicial building for some years after it was deconsecrated in 1835. Today, the cloister and pillared arcades are home to the town's ★★ **fruit and vegetable market**, plus a number of shops selling leather goods and craft work. The ecclesiastical architecture and the intense colours and smells of a Mediterranean market make an an unusual mixture. In the centre of the cloister, concerts are often performed on summer evenings.

On the small Plaça de la Mirandea beyond the church, in a fine and commanding position above the harbour, is a monument to Almirante Augusto Miranda, honoured with a bust, an anchor and a cannon for having founded the naval station at Maó in 1916. From here you can follow the curved road or the broad steps of Costa de Ses Voltes, lined by shrubs and palms, to the harbour spread out below.

THE HARBOUR

Local people refer to their harbour simply as ★★ **Es Port** ❿, and it is undoubtedly the biggest attraction of the island's capital. This natural harbour is 6km (4 miles) long and up to 1km (½ mile) across. Maó was considered the safest harbour in the Mediterranean by Andrea Doria, Admiral of the Spanish Navy. But in the years since its naval days – the British kept most of their Mediterranean fleet here until 1802 – the harbour has had to earn its living in different ways.

The mariners' pubs and dives have been turned into elegant restaurants, bars and discos and the **Baixamar** is now the busiest promenade in town. Instead of destroyers, cruise ships, ferries and freighters visit the harbour and the jetty is lined by hundreds of white-sailed yachts from all over the world, all contributing to a picturesque scene.

Below: local sailors
Bottom: Mediterranean cruise-liner

BOAT TOUR

The best way of getting a view of Maó from the sea is to take a round trip of the harbour. Glass-bottomed boats depart from the main harbour area

Map on page 24

Sampling the gin

The Xoriguer Distillery (open daily; closed 1–4pm) produces gin and various gin-based liqueurs in its old-fashioned copper stills. Gin has been made on Menorca since the late 18th century, but its popularity with British sailors helped ensure its survival. Visitors are encouraged to taste and buy; try the gin-and-lemonade mix, *pomada*, a Menorcan version of gin-and-tonic .

Below: hanging out in Maó
Bottom: gin was introduced by the British

on an hourly basis in summer. The trip leads past the **Illa del Rei**, or King's Island, with its former naval hospital, and the **Illa Quarantena** with the ruins of the medieval quarantine station. The Illa d'es Llazteret at the exit of the bay once served as a plague island during an outbreak of the deadly disease; today the hospital is used as a holiday home. The harbour could quickly be sealed off in times of danger, as is clear from the ruins of the fortress of Sant Felip near Es Castell and the La Mola fortress on the Cap de la Mola opposite. The latter is still used by the Spanish army and is out of bounds. Until 1968 it was one of the most notorious military prisons of the Franco era.

Not far from here is the so-called **Nelson Museum**, a rusty-red colonial manor house in best 18th-century colonial style above the northern part of the harbour bay. The house and its luxuriant grounds are jointly known as Golden Farm. Despite the name, the house is not a museum; it is privately owned and cannot be visited. The popular story connecting the place with Admiral Horatio Nelson (1758–1805) is equally misleading. Although legend has it that Nelson spent several romantic weeks here with his mistress, Lady Emma Hamilton, the truth is that he made just one brief visit to Menorca – and he was alone.

ATTRACTIONS FOR ALL AGES

Back to the harbour now, where the numerous and varied restaurants are joined by fashion and ceramic shops. In the **Alfarería Menorquina** (Moll de Ponent 10; May–Oct, daily 9am–9pm, Jul–Aug till 11pm) you can look over the shoulder of a woman potter as she works, and there's a parrot, too, to amuse the children. Other children's highlights at the harbour include the *Acuario*, at Moll de Ponent 73, a pub whose landlord charges steep prices for visits to his aquarium with turtles, lobsters and sea-snakes.

Adults prefer the **Destileria Xoriguer** (Moll de Ponent 93), which distils and sells the only gin on Menorca. The crush for the gin begins early in the morning when the first cruise boats dock.

EXCURSIONS FROM MAÓ

Apart from Maó's main beach, the Cala Mesquida and the dreamy little bay of Cala Murtar (both to the north of Cap de la Mola), there are some other attractive destinations near the city.

Star Attraction
• **Ermita de Gracia**

ERMITA DE GRACIA

The ★★ **Ermita de Gracia** and the municipal **Cimenterio**, both on the southwestern edge of Maó, can be reached after a longish walk.

The unpretentious monastery church was built between 1436 and 1491 and consecrated to the Virgin Mary, but was used for all kinds of purposes after that. First it was utilised as a military hospital by the French and then the Spanish, and in the 18th century it even contained a powder magazine. The snow-white façade dates from 1733, and the nave is Gothic. The maritime votive offerings inside were donated by mariners and fishermen rescued from shipwrecks; they were especially grateful to Nostra Senyora de Gracia, whose statue can be seen in a niche behind the altar.

The peaceful cemetery, with its rows of tombs, is also worth a visit. Anyone who could afford to do so had veritable palaces built above their tombs, as a mark of their prestige.

Below: Cala Mesquida
Bottom: Ermita de Gracia

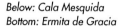

Map
on page
49

TREPUCO

It is less than 2km (1 mile) from the church to the megalithic settlement of **Trepucó**. The *talayot* (fortified tower) here is one of the largest on Menorca, and the *taula* (table-shaped stone) is certainly the most magnificent pre-Christian sacred monument on the Balearic Islands. The supporting stone is 4.2m (13.7ft) high and covered by a 3.5m (11.5ft) by 1.5m (5ft) stone slab; there are also numerous menhirs scattered around the temple site.

ES CASTELL

Below: taula at Trepucó
Bottom: life in Es Castell

★★ **Es Castell** (pop. 5,400), located on the southern edge of Maó's broad harbour, is certainly worth devoting a whole day to. It has two inlets, Cala Fonts and Cala Corb, and is the most easterly town in Spain and the first to get the morning sun. It was founded in the late 18th century when the British built a garrison town near the fortress of Sant Felip and named it Georgetown, after George III. Under the Spanish it became Real Villa de San Carlos (Villa Carlos), in honour of the king of Spain. Finally the present name, which simply means The Castle, stuck, because of its proximity to the fortress.

As in Maó, life in Es Castell revolves around a central square that was a former parade ground. The town's history is reflected in the architecture here. The square is lined by the Ajuntament (Town Hall), a barracks containing the **Museu Militar de Menorca** (Sat–Sun 11am–1pm), and numerous cafés and bars.

Inviting café terraces also line the beautiful bay of Cala Fonts, which has all the atmosphere and charm of a fishing-harbour. Many of the shops and restaurants are built into caves in the walls around the harbour, with a wide range of items on sale, from ceramics to *abarcas*, the traditional Menorquin sandals, all in a relaxing setting. You can also visit **Fort Marlborough** (Tues–Sat 10am–1pm, 5–8pm, Sun 10am–1pm) an 18th-century British fort with a Martello tower and underground galleries.

2: Ciutadella

Ciutadella, Menorca's former capital, is very different from British-influenced Maó. Large, splendid *palazzi* and an impressive cathedral are as much a part of the scene here as shady arcades, beautiful sun-soaked squares and an undeniably picturesque harbour.

The ★★★ **Old Town** of Ciutadella was built in the 16th and 17th centuries, after a 15,000-strong Turkish army had completely destroyed all previous structures, and it is remarkably homogeneous. An obelisk in the Plaça d'es Born commemorates the Turkish attack. This broad square is lined with bars where you can stop for a *ginebra* – the Menorcan gin – or relax over a *café con leche*.

Ciutadella (pop. 21,000) is a fascinating place. Its narrow alleyways are so tempting that it's very easy to ignore maps and guidebooks and simply set off exploring alone. Wherever you end up is bound to be pleasant and you are unlikely to get lost for long.

HISTORY

The town's origins date back to the Phoenicians, who founded a trading post in the west of the island and called it *Iamnona*. They were followed

Map on page 36

Star Attraction
• Es Castell

Menorca's Little City
As the crow flies, Ciutadella is less than 50km (30 miles) from the Mallorcan coast; at dusk the mountains of Mallorca turn pink on the horizon. So perhaps it should come as no surprise that the old town, with its Gothic churches and honey-stone façades, is rather like a miniature Palma. This is, after all, what the city's name implies. Palma's alternative name is Ciutat de Mallorca; Ciutadella de Menorca means 'Menorca's little city'.

Ciutadella kids

by the Romans, and the settlement was fortified and extended, but for a long time it lay in the shadow of *Portus Magonis*, today's Maó, in the east of the island. For a short while in the 5th century, Ciutadella was one of the first bishoprics in the Balearic Islands.

When the Moors took over power the town became known as *Medina Minurka*, and as capital of the island it was the seat of the Arab governor for centuries. In 1287 the Christian king Alfonso III of Aragón entered the city via the Porto de Maó, today's Plaça de Alfons III *(see page 47)* after a three-day victorious march, and named it Ciutadella de Menorca, which means Menorca's little city.

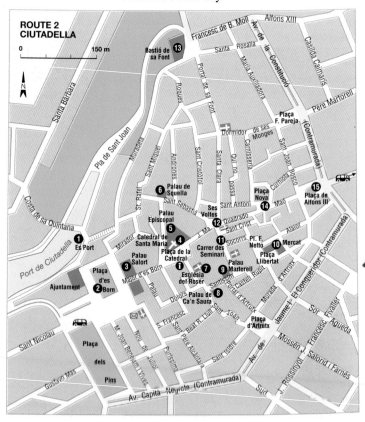

ROUTE 2
CIUTADELLA

0   150 m

N

RISEN FROM THE ASHES

New town walls and bastions now appeared, based on the fortifications at Perpignan, and attacks by Moorish and Turkish pirates could at first be repelled. A black day in the town's history was 9 July 1558: after nine and a half days' siege, a 15,000-strong Turkish army entered Ciutadella, plundering and murdering, and finally leaving with 3,500 hostages. All that remained of the town was dust and ash.

This is why the reconstruction in the 17th century was more like a re-foundation. Magnificent *palazzi* were built in the Catalan and Italian styles. But in the meantime, Maó was becoming increasingly important for military reasons, and in 1722 the British turned Ciutadella's rival into the island's capital. To soothe ruffled feelings, Ciutadella was made a bishopric in 1795. In the mid-19th century large sections of the town's fortifications were razed to the ground to make way for more residential land. Today the town lives from the leather and shoe-making industry as well as from tourism, and the harbour is only of regional importance.

THE FESTA DE SANT JOAN

The Festa de Sant Joan, which takes place each year on 23–24 June, is celebrated all over Spain, but nowhere with such raucous abandon as in Ciutadella. On the previous Sunday, a live ram is carried around the town on the shoulders of a man dressed in sheepskins, representing John the Baptist. Then, for two days, the citizens of Ciutadella go wild, with crowds of people thronging into Plaça d'es Born and neighbouring streets to witness horseback processions, firework displays and jousting tournaments.

Most of the rituals enacted here revolve around the Menorcan passion for horses, and the *caixers*, or horsemen, who represent the medieval social classes, ride among the crowds, prancing and circling on their horses' hind legs. The longer a horse manages to stay on two legs, the greater the roaring appreciation of the crowd, which surges

Shopping for shoes
Ciutadella's shoe industry has been well known even beyond the island's shores ever since the late 19th century. Locally made shoes can be bought in numerous outlets in the city centre as well as on the outskirts (towards Maó and Cala en Bosc).

Below: weekly market
Bottom: Bastió de sa Font

Map on page 36

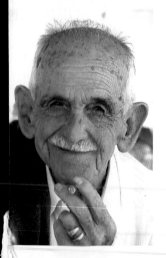

Exploring on foot
The best way to explore Ciutadella is to walk, with an accurate map but no fixed route, at different times of the day and night. Inevitably you keep returning to the streets around the cathedral. At night, history comes alive here, with small architectural details – sundials, saints in niches, coats of arms – spotlighted by old-fashioned street lamps. By this time the fish restaurants beside the port are starting to fill up, but if you walk back along the creek and look up at the old wall, you can imagine past centuries, when the gates were locked from sunset to sunrise.

Veteran of the times

forward, trying to get as close as possible to the action. It may look as though some of the braver revellers are in imminent danger of being trampled underfoot, but the horses are light footed and very well trained. Daredevil antics also apply to the jousting, where the idea is for the rider to spear a hoop hanging from a wire in the middle of the square. The expectant crowd first closes in on the horse and rider, only parting at the last minute as they gallop at full speed towards the hoop, and then closing ranks again once they have passed. A successfully speared hoop is met with another roar of appreciation.

When night falls, the horses and riders have another task to perform: they trot around town calling in at people's homes and receiving a welcoming drink, an activity that is said to bring luck to the hospitable household.

CENTRAL SIGHTS

There is always something rather seductive about harbour towns, and this is definitely true of ★★ **Es Port ❶**, Ciutadella's harbour . The long narrow bay to which the British decided not to entrust their ships is utterly Mediterranean in character. The quays are almost overflowing with the chairs on the café terraces and bars, which have names like El Bribón or Es Moll. Skippers of all nationalities meet up here each evening for a few *copas* and *tapas* while their white yachts are lined up nearby, easily outnumbering the fishing boats.

A glass-bottomed boat awaits passengers for extended trips along the coast. The local fishermen can be seen sitting outside the Café Balear, the news centre of Ciutadella, from early morning onwards. The attractive backdrop to this scene is provided by the ochre-coloured town wall, with the fortified former Town Hall rising above it.

As you stroll along the harbour you will see a rocky outcrop with the **Castell de Sant Nicolau** on top – an octagonal defensive tower dating from the 17th century that once protected the harbour. Today it contains a museum (May–Oct, Mon–Sat 7.30am–9.30pm) with old photographs and engravings, as well as several informative boards depicting historical events. A bust outside commemorates David Glasgow Farragut (1801–70), the son of a captain from Ciutadella, who fought in the American Civil War and then conquered New Orleans and rose to become the first four-star admiral of the United States. When he visited his father's town in 1867, he was given a hero's welcome, with huge crowds lining the streets.

Star Attractions
• **Es Port**
• **Plaça d'es Born**

PLAÇA D'ES BORN

The steps of the small alleyway, Capllonch, lead past souvenir stands and boutiques to the ★★ **Plaça d'es Born ❷**, the beating heart of the town, and the scene every June of the Festa de Sant Joan *(see page 37)*. This pretty square is bordered by the former Town Hall and the finest *palazzi* in Ciutadella, and looks lovely at night when illuminated by the soft light from the wrought-iron street lamps.

In the middle of the square, around the obelisk commemorating those who fell in the Ottoman attack of 1558, a lively market is held every Friday and Saturday selling textiles, jewellery and Far Eastern items. From the **Bastió des Port**, the northern side of the square, there's a magnificent panoramic view of the harbour. Next door is the Cercle Artístic cafe, an art association in

Below: Plaça d'es Born
Bottom: Ciutadella harbour

Map on page 36

Hallowed hall

The neo-Gothic council hall inside the Ajuntament has several familial coats of arms on its wooden ceiling as well as portraits of illustrious Menorcans around the walls. You will probably only be able to see it on 9 July every year an account of the terrible attack on the city in 1558 by the Turks is read aloud in the hall.

existence since 1881 – a good place to meet local people or simply sit back in a soft leather chair and enjoy a morning cup of coffee. The **Teatre Municipal d'es Born** shows films every evening, and plays are frequently performed here, too.

The imposing building with high battlements that dominates the western end of the Plaça is still known as the **Ajuntament** (Town Hall), although it is now the police headquarters. There was once a Moorish castle on this site, then a fortress, constructed by Alfonso III in the 13th century. Today's building, which dates from the 19th century, has a colourful floor mosaic in front of the main entrance showing the municipal coat of arms, in which the blue of the Mediterranean and the grey-brown of several impregnable-looking battlements predominate.

GRAND PALACES

The magnificence of the opposite side of the square is hard to beat: from right to left stand the **palaces** of the Saura, Salort and Vivó families, with their richly decorated façades. Time is taking its toll, however. The ground floors contain cafés and souvenir shops, and a Burger King outlet is vying for custom with the specialities of Menorcan cuisine. As the descendants of the noble families now live in Barcelona or Madrid

Saura Palace

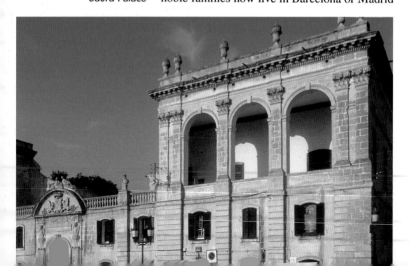

and only make brief visits during the summer, the shutters on the upper storeys are usually closed.

The **Palau de Torre Saura**, with its two wings, has a mighty portal with a coat of arms set into it, a magnificent inner courtyard, fine loggias and even Renaissance-style *putti* on the roof. The only one of the palaces that can be visited is the splendid **Palau de Salort ❸** (May–Sept, Mon–Sat 10am–2pm), built in 1813, with one of its side wings facing the square, and the entrance at the side in Carrer Major del Born. It contains not only a ballroom and a mirror hall but also bedchambers and a historic kitchen. Alongside antique furniture, numerous paintings and family portraits, as well as several valuable tapestries, there is also a fine Buick dating from the 1920s.

Below: Saura Palace detail
Bottom: the cathedral

The noble façade of the **Palau Vivó** is decorated by oriel windows and balconies and the atrium contains a magnificent double staircase, but unfortunately it is closed to visitors.

SANTA MARIA CATHEDRAL

The Carrer Major del Born leads between the *palazzi* – note the finely worked door-knockers with sea serpents and women's heads – to the **Plaça de la Catedral**, where the helpful tourist office is located and entertainers keep the crowds amused. The most prominent structure in this square, and the most important religious building in Menorca, is the single-aisled, square-cut ★ **Catedral de Santa Maria ❹** (daily 8am–1pm, 6.30–9pm). Begun around 1300, after the Moors had been driven from the island, it was built on the site of an earlier mosque, as were so many churches on the islands. Its bell-tower was once a minaret, and *marés* – the porous sandstone of Menorca – gives the cathedral its warm, golden-brown colour.

When the Turks invaded the town in 1558 they also plundered and destroyed this building. In 1795, after a great deal of intensive repair work, it was elevated to the status of a cathedral when a papal edict gave Ciutadella a bishop.

The façade is dominated by the neo-classical main portal, which dates from 1814. The original

Port de la Llum, or door of light, from the 14th century, is decorated with a relief showing magnificent, fabled creatures and the coat of arms of Aragón and Ciutadella. The first thing you will notice when you go inside is the warm light falling through the colourful stained-glass windows. The 12 side chapels are also striking: most of them date from the Renaissance era, as does the Catalan Gothic main altar. The money for the altar and the church bells was donated by Alfonso III, while the rather plain-looking but melodious organ was consecrated in 1993 in the presence of the present Spanish king, Juan Carlos I.

Below: Palau de Olivar
Bottom: detail from
Església del Roser

EPISCOPAL DELIGHTS

Opposite the main portal of the Cathedral is the neo-classical Palau de Olivar, which, like so many other *palazzi* in Ciutadella, is not open to visitors. At the 18th-century **Palau Episcopal** (Episcopal Palace) ❺ in the Carrer de Ca'l Bisbe there is at least a quiet inner courtyard that can be visited (9am–noon) and which connects the palace and the Cathedral. There is a fine view of the bell-tower, and benches in the garden on which to sit and relax.

The loggia-like entrance to the palace is Italian-influenced, and a tile picture on the Cathedral wall shows the *Madonna of Monte Toro*. Local people used to collect water from the well here, which now has a grille over the top and no longer contains water.

In the Carrer Sant Sebastià, a few steps further on, the golden stucco work on the **Palau de Squella** ❻ glints in the sunshine. In 1867 this is where the Admiral David Glasgow Farragut, hero of the American War of Independence and son of an emigrant from Ciutadella, stayed when he visited the island in 1867 *(see page 39)*.

Opposite the Porta de la Llum, the Cathedral's south door, narrow Carrer del Roser branches off, leading towards **Església del Roser** ❼, which dates from the 17th and 18th centuries. Its baroque façade has a striking entrance, its pillars, adorned with artistic flower, fruit and leaf ornamentation. Since the apse collapsed in 1977 and restoration work began, the church no longer holds services. However, the **Sala Municipal d'Exposicions El Roser** is a good venue today for chamber music evenings and art exhibitions.

TWO PALACES

A few metres further on, in Carrer Santíssim, is the **Palau de Ca'n Saura ❽**, another townhouse owned by the once influential Saura family. The *palazzo*, which took just one year to build in 1697, has recently been restored. The clear lines of the façade, the windows and the projecting roof reveal the feeling for form and the craftsmanship of the island's master architects of that era. If you can get inside, which unfortunately is seldom possible, there is an impressive staircase and several Roman amphorae to admire.

The **Palau Martorell ❾** directly opposite is every bit as attractive, but is always closed to the public. Locally, this 17th-century building is referred to merely as the *Cas Duc*, or Duke's House; the exterior has striking semi-circular balconies and deep-set windows.

A VISIT TO THE MARKET

Things get noisy and busy again at the end of the Carrer del Castell Rupit on the arcaded Plaça

Below: local advert
Bottom: C'al Bisbe

de la Libertat, and there are some fascinating aromas in the air. In the morning (Tues–Sat) the ★★ **Mercat** (Market) ❿ is held here. The small 18th-century pavilion is filled with stands of seafood and fish, and beyond the wide-open doors of the green-and-white-tiled market hall opposite there are mountains of meat and sausage for sale.

Around the market are numerous bars like the Piscolabis or the Ulises, where the clientele is almost always entirely local. Some of them live in the old people's home in the nearby Carrer de l'Hospital de Santa Magdalena, where the pensioners live not only in the middle of town but right in the middle of life too.

In the Casa de Cultura opposite, young men and women can be seen walking to and fro from the music school with heavy instrument cases; there is also a well-stocked town library here (the books are mainly in Spanish but there are also sections with English, French and German titles).

CARRER DES SEMINARI

The **Carrer des Seminari** ⓫ is a cultural and historical monument of the first degree. When you emerge from Carrer del Sant Christ you will find yet another souvenir of the Saura family immediately on the right: the unpretentious **Palau de Saura** was built by an 18th-century British governor for Joan Miquel Saura, who took the Habsburg side against the Bourbons in the War of the Spanish Succession and forfeited his house as a result. The ground floor is occupied by a branch of the Caixa de Catalunya savings bank, which is funding extensive restoration work.

Next door is the **Església del Socors**, which was once part of an Augustinian monastery destroyed by the Turks and rebuilt in the 17th century. The twin-towered Renaissance church was begun in 1648. Today it serves as the auditorium for the music conservatory of the Capilla Davidica, so it is not open to the public except on special occasions when concerts are held in the **Seminar Concilar** – the only opportunity to study the rather damaged but still fine ceiling frescoes.

Below: fish in the market
Bottom: exploring the backstreets

There is a soaring cloister and a pretty monastery garden with lemon trees and a well, which was laid out between 1616 and 1676, and restored in the 1990s. The hallowed halls contain a priests' seminary, and there is also a library here, together with the small **Museu Diocesà** (Diocesan Museum; May–Oct, Tues–Sat 10.30am–1.30pm), which not only has a large collection of prehistoric archaeological finds and ecclesiastical artefacts but also some landscape paintings by the Catalan artist Pere Daura (1896–1976), who was born in Ciutadella.

SHOPPING STREET

If you turn on your heel at this point there are several pleasant boutiques to discover on the other side of the street, selling hand-made bags, lampshades and Malayan sarongs. Alternatively you could try a *horchata* – a sweet milky drink made from ground almonds – at the Café Paradis while admiring the portal of the monastery.

At the other end of the street is the **Església del Sant Christ**, which dates from 1667. It contains an unusual painting, the *Christ dels Peraires*. In the 17th century, beads of perspiration are said to have appeared on Christ's face in the painting, which is why the work is so treasured today.

Star Attraction
• Mercat

Eye for detail
When you visit the Diocesan Museum, be sure to take a look at the neo-classical door in the boundary wall. It is crowned by an odd sculpture of the Virgin Mary, threatening a dragon-devil with a hammer and cudgel.

Seminar Concilar ceiling

UNDERNEATH THE ARCHES

On the triangular Plaça Vella, a column with the flag of the Knights of St John commemorates Ciutadella's famous festival, the Festes de Sant Joan *(see page 37)*. There is also a plaque here commemorating the birth of Josep Maria Quadrado (1819–96). He lived in Mallorca in his later life and became famous as a novelist and historian who spoke out strongly in favour of Catalan as a literary language.

Below: Crucifixion, Sant Christ
Bottom: Municipal Museum

The Carrer de Sant Josep leads across the tiny and delightful square known as ★★**Ses Voltes** (The Arches) ⑫, This was a local nickname that has now been adopted officially. There are deep Gothic-style arcades in the white buildings on either side where you can window-shop or just enjoy the cool shade on a hot day.

Some marvellous tourist-oriented shops include *confiterias* (sweet shops), *pastellerias* (pastry shops), fashion and shoe shops and there are café tables out in the centre of the square. This is a spot you can fall in love with very quickly.

THE MUNICIPAL MUSEUM

From here, make a detour along the Carrer de Santa Clara, a street full of jewellery shops, to the town's fortifications. This area is the oldest in Ciutadella. The Palau de Lluriac, with its pillared windows, was formerly yet another property of the Salort family and today houses the offices of the island's main newspaper, although the adjoining 17th-century Convent de Santa Clara is still inhabited by nuns.

At the end of the street, the stocky-looking ★**Bastió de sa Font** ⑬ was built between 1677 and 1692 and is part of the few remains of Ciutadella's former fortifications. The **Museu Municipal** (Mar–Sept, Tues–Sat 10am–2pm) is housed here and its numerous vaulted rooms contain a rich collection of archaeological finds from all epoch's of the island's history, as well as interesting models of megalithic villages. There is also a vaulted antechamber that is used for art exhibitions in the summer.

PLAÇA NOVA

On the way back towards the centre, you could visit the **Casa-Museu del Pintor Torrent** (May–Oct, daily 11am–1pm, 7.30–9.30pm) devoted to the work of the painter born in Ciutadella in 1904, who has been called 'the Menorcan Van Gogh'.

From here, continue to Ses Voltes, then on to the well-patronised ★ **Plaça Nova** . This is where the people of Ciutadella like to gather, and if you want to join them, simply take a seat outside the Café Xoriguer or at the cafeteria Al Arco and watch the world go by.

If you have time and energy before embarking on the nightlife in the harbour quarter, take a stroll through the pedestrian precinct and look at the houses and shops on the Camí de Maó with their beautiful wrought-iron balconies.

In the palm-tree-lined **Plaça de Alfons III** ⑮, known locally as the **Plaça de Ses Palmeres** (Square of the Palm Trees), you will see people feeding swarms of ever-hungry pigeons.

On the far side of the square, the **Museu Molí des Comtes** (Jun–Sept, Tues–Sun 10am–1pm), housed in an attractive white 18th-century windmill, displays machinery and other milling artefacts. Adjoining it, in what was the old grain store, is a group of artisan enterprises, a small tourist office, public toilets and access to a car park.

Star Attraction
• Ses Voltes

Cranial surgery
Some of the ancient skulls on view in the Museu Municipal show wounds caused by trepanning in cranial surgery, which indicate that the *talyotic* culture must have developed advanced surgical techniques. In some cases the wounds have healed over, proving, somewhat remarkably, that the patients must have survived.

Plaça Nova

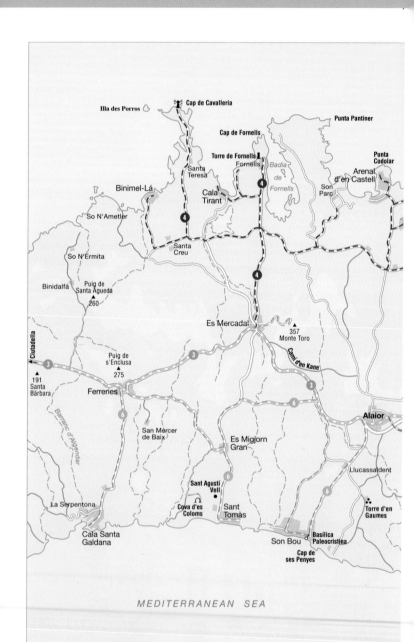

ROUTES 3 - 6

0   3 km

MEDITERRANEAN SEA

Na Macaret

Cap de Favàritx

Port
d'Addaia

④

Morella
Vell

Illa d'en Colom

④

S'Albufera

Es
Grau

Punta de sa Galera

Sant
Llorenç

④

Cala
Mesquida

Camí d'en Kane

④

Sant
Antoni

Cala
Llonga

Punta de
s'Esperó

Torralba
d'en Salort

Rafal Rubí

③

Mahón

Es
Castell

Illa d'es
Llatzaret

Santa
Ana

Cap de
la Mola

Son Seguí

Algendar

Talatí
de Dalt

Torrellonet

⑤

Sant
Llorenç

Trebalúger

Binissaida

Torre
Llisà
Vell

So Na
Caçana

Sant
Climent

Llucmaçanes

Calaen
Porter

Binicalaf

Biniparrell

Sant
Lluís

S'Algar

Sant
Eloi

Son Vitamina
del Mar

⑤

S'Ullastrar

Torret

Cala
d'Alcaufar

Cales
Coves

Es Canutells

Binissafúller

Biniancolla

Binidali

Cap
d'en Font

Binibeca
Vell

Cala
Torret

⑤

Punta
Prima

Illa de l'Aire

Map
on pages
48–9

3: Along the Island Axis

Maó – Alaior – Es Mercadal – Monte Toro – Puig de Santa Agueda – Naveta d'es Tudons – Ciutadella (88km/54 miles)

The road from Maó to Ciutadella runs along the backbone of Menorca. Other roads branch off it to coves, beaches and villages and also to the tourist centres – some are bumpy, narrow, and full of recently filled potholes, while others might be easy-to-miss tracks leading to prehistoric sites, fields of scrub and cactus or country estates. You will have to keep returning to this road to get around the island, because instead of a coast road, Menorca merely has an old horse track, the Camí de Cavalls *(see page 11)*.

👁 Camí d'en Kane

If you have time, it's well worth getting to know the 16km (10 miles) or so that still survive of this old route across Menorca. The narrow, bendy road leads repeatedly past *parets seques*, those dry walls so typical of the island, remote farms, rich green meadows or oak groves. Sometimes ancient pine trees form avenues.

The Camí d'en Kane starts on the Maó–Fornells road at Km 3.6, rounds the cemetery outside Alaior, and comes out onto the C721 just before Es Mercadal. A further 4-km (2-mile) section can be found north-west of the town in the direction of Ferreries, but it ends in tracks and eventually at the main road again.

JOURNEY OF DISCOVERY

Towns to discover to the right and left of the main Menorcan highway include Alaior, Es Mercadal and Ferreries, all of which have grown very slowly since the 14th century. All have parish churches, narrow streets and pretty squares with cafés and restaurants. There are also the ancient Navetes de Rafal Rubi, the Naveta d'es Tudons and the Taula Torre Trencada, all built during an unparalleled period of construction some 3,500 years ago. Finally, the quiet charm of Menorca can best be appreciated during the early morning or early evening hours from the top of Monte Toro (357m/1,170ft), the highest 'mountain' on the island, with its breathtaking all-round panoramic view.

LEAVING MAO

Leave Maó on the C721, the main road across the island, in a westerly direction and you will first find yourself travelling through the large commercial area of the capital. Yachts, motorboats and diving suits are on sale here, and there are outlets selling Spanish wines or glazed ceramics in every imaginable colour. Just beyond the point where the road branches away to the airport a

Cycling the Camí d'en Kane

small road leads off to the left, to two attractions that no visitor to Menorca should miss.

The ★ **Sansuguet Estate** is where the Menorcan-born painter Francisco Sans Huguet set up a magnificent refuge for himself in 1926, after years of wandering through Europe and holding exhibitions in many of the great museums of Paris, Madrid and Toledo. The whole house contains Huguet's works, and visitors are only allowed in if a member of his family is present. If they manage to get talking, there's usually a glass of red straight from the barrel, and the afternoon can become a long one. The paintings and drawings all around the house are signed with the artist's pseudonym 'Sansuguet', and alongside still-lifes and portraits and accurately rendered scenes from Paris or Toledo, there are a large number of Menorcan landscapes.

Below: Sansuguet Estate
Bottom: Navetes
de Rafal Rubí

TALATI DE DALT

A frequently recurring motif with Huguet is located right outside his front door: the megalithic settlement of **Talati de Dalt**, just a stone's throw away and surrounded by gnarled mastic trees, olive trees and carobs. It was inhabited until Roman times, and is considered to be one of the better-preserved ancient sites of Menorca. Stone steps lead over a wall into the village, which, with

Map
on pages
48–9

its *taula* and *talayot*, weathered circle of stones and caves, still gives us a very good impression of a prehistoric settlement. The *taula* is enclosed in a circular plot of land. A stone column leans against it, seeming to support the table-shaped structure.

From the high *talayot* there is a fine view of the surrounding area, and of the maze of stone walls across the island. The present and the past sit side by side: nearby, the Talayot Torelló is visible, and at the airport charter planes can be seen landing and taking off. If you happen to be visiting Menorca in the springtime, there will be wild flowers blooming everywhere: red poppies, mauve, yellow and white crocuses and knee-high thistles with purple flowers.

Below: Talati de Dalt
Bottom: pointing the way

MEGALITHIC STRUCTURES

Since there are roughly two prehistoric sites per square kilometre on this island, you'll make very slow headway if you want to visit each one. Just 1.5km (1 mile) further on you can leave the main road again and visit the *talayots* of **Binaiet Vell** on a small rise to the right, plus the prehistoric site of **Sant Vicent d'Acaidús**. The highlights of this village are two *circuli* – buildings on a circular ground-plan that were used as living accommodation 2,500 years ago.

The ★ **Navetes de Rafal Rubí** can be found in a field to the right of the road. These megalithic structures, formerly family tombs, resemble overturned boats. Archaeological finds here have dated their origin to around 1500BC. A narrow track that also leads to the parallel Camí d'en Kane (*see page 50*) will take you to a rickety wooden gate, leading to a field and to the first and best-preserved of the *navetas*. If you crawl inside the low doorway you will see the antechamber and several more rooms. Light penetrates through several cracks, and also through the larger *naveta* nearby. Using the simplest of means, the stones were carefully placed side by side here – and so densely that not even a hand can fit through the cracks.

navetes d'enterrament
de Rafal Rubí

ALAIOR

Next comes the third-largest town on Menorca and also its cheesemaking centre: ★★ **Alaior** (pop. 6,400). Most of the cheese known as *Queso de Mahón* and marketed in the capital is actually made here. Whole cheeses or sections can be bought from wholesalers or at cooperatives such as Coinga or Quesos Torralba, or from the small shop opposite the La Payesa factory (past Plaça de Sant Francesc). The factory itself cannot be visited, but it can be smelled as you approach.

This pretty town has other attractions besides its cheese, however. To get a good view of unwelcome guests, it was built on a hilltop. The narrow streets and house façades are definitely worth a closer look; with its colourful houses and window frames, Alaior comes across as generally far more colourful than other towns on Menorca.

GEM OF A COURTYARD

One real gem is the ★★ **Plaça de Sant Francesc**, an interior courtyard surrounded by four-storey buildings that once belonged to the neighbouring Franciscan Convent de Sant Diego. Its inhabitants refer to it poetically as *Pati de san Lluna*, or Courtyard of the Moon. With its fine galleries, its well and its dangling potted plants, this courtyard has a wonderfully light atmosphere that coun-

Star Attractions
•Alaior
Plaça de Sant Francesc

Below: local cheese
Bottom: Alaior

teracts the severity of its geometrical architecture. The Convent de Sant Diego itself is now a **Centre Cultural** (Wed–Fri 10am–1pm, 6–9pm, Tues 6–9pm, Sat 10am–1pm) which holds exhibitions with artesan and rural themes.

The nearby church of **Santa Eulalia** has a plain exterior and the decoration inside is also very restrained. At the end of the 17th century this massive church replaced a previous structure, built when the town was founded by Jaume II in the 14th century.

REPRESENTATIVE BUILDINGS

In the narrow Carrer Major, the **Palau Salort** is highly reminiscent of one of the feudal *palazzi* of Ciutadella. Obviously the people of Alaior weren't inclined to leave all the representative buildings to the island's former capital.

Opposite is the **Casa Consistorial**, which is another name for Ajuntament (Town Hall). Built in 1612, later than the town halls of Ciutadella and Maó, it is the finest on the island. The façade has an elaborately decorated balcony and even more decorative flags.

It's worth taking a look behind the façade here where you'll see a magnificent flight of steps, elegant patio and comprehensive collection of paintings centred on regional historical events. One real highlight is the Gothic painting *Rei Jaume II de Mallorca* by Miguel Alejandre. Art exhibitions are regularly held on the first floor of the building, as well.

Two views of Alaior cemetery

CEMETERY

While in Alaior you could visit the ★★ **cemetery**, situated 1.5km (1 mile) north of the town. Cemeteries are not everyone's idea of a tourist site, of course, but the niche graves set close together, monumental tombs and well-tended white funerary chapels are quite splendid.

On the way to the cemetery you can also look at the road known as Es Cós, which was used as a racecourse during British rule here. It is lined to right and left by white-painted benches where spectators used to sit. The grandstand can be made out just to the left of the cemetery. This was where the town worthies used to sit and a small flight of steps led up to it. The Camí d'en Kane *(see page 50)*, the old cross-island route used by the British, also leads past the cemetery.

DETOUR TO ERMITA DE SANT LLORENC

Since you are travelling eastwards there's a worthwhile detour at this point to the ★ **Ermita de Sant Llorenc de Binixems**. A bumpy track leads off to the left, passing remote farms and quarries to arrive at one of the oldest churches on the island. Its existence has been dated back to the early 14th century. After its destruction by an earthquake in 1654, it was rebuilt in the Renaissance style, but in 1898 it had become so dilapidated that it had to be renovated at great expense. And there it stands alone, surrounded by fields of grazing cows.

> **Festival time**
> The Ermita de Sant Llorenc is often closed, but things get very busy once a year during the festival of St Laurence, which takes place in mid-August. A procession of riders from Alaior comes and visits the church. The saint can be seen in a medallion above the main door.

ES MERCADAL

If you continue westwards along the main road now you'll reach the **Es Puig Mal**, or Mountain of Evil – so watch your driving. Here the road reaches its highest elevation of 200m (720ft), and

Es Mercadal from above

Map
on pages
48–9

Es Mercadal specialities
Most of the cooks in Es Mercadal specialise in Menorcan cuisine: for example, the owner of the Ca n'Aguedet restaurant has even brought back viticulture to the island and is now the exclusive provider of genuine Menorcan wine. The small almond macaroons known as *amargos* are also utterly delicious. Es Mercadal is also famous for shoes: the *avarques* (leather sandals with soles made of of tyres), are made in this region.

from now on Monte Toro, which provides the very best all-round view of the island, is constantly in sight until the town of ★ **Es Mercadal** (pop. 2,400) appears at its feet.

Brilliantly white houses contrast with the green of the surrounding landscape, giving this 700-year-old municipality its striking appearance. Es Mercadal's popularity derives not only from its central location as a starting-point for hikes across the Monte Toro region but also from the excellent food served here, which has a high reputation throughout the island.

HISTORIC CISTERN

The largely dry river bed of the Torrente makes it clear why one 18th-century structure is important to the people of Es Mercadal: the *aljub*. This 20m by 40m (65ft by 130ft) cistern, which is 9m (30ft) deep, was built at the behest of governor Richard Kane between 1736 and 1740. The English governor had noticed the connection between the water shortage and the frequent diseases on the island, and financed the construction out of his own pocket. Today the cistern is still opened on Saturday morning. That's when the local people take their buckets or canisters along and take a few litres of chlorine-free rain water home with them – but not without having caught up on the latest gossip, of course.

18th-century cistern,
Es Mercadal

MONTE TORO

From now on the views get spectacular, along the road full of hairpin bends that leads up to the ★★★ **Monte Toro** (357m/1,170ft), or along the hiking routes to the top. After a good hour's walk you will find yourself confronted by a stunning, all-round view from the top of Menorca's highest peak. It extends from the Cap de Cavalleria in the west to the beaches of the south coast – and on clear days you can even make out Mallorca in the distance without a problem. This sacred peak is crowned by a massive statue of Christ, next door to a forest of radio and television antennae. The statue is spreading his arms out to bless the Menorcans who fell during the Spanish wars in Morocco.

Star Attraction
• **Monte Toro**

ANCIENT CENTRE OF PILGRIMAGE

There used to be a Gothic Augustinian monastery on this peak called the Santuari de la Mare de Deu del Toro, and it was the spiritual centre of the island. A baroque-style pilgrimage church dating from the 17th century now stands on the same site, beside a hermitage (accommodation available by prior arrangement, tel: 971 37 50 60) and the remains of a defensive tower. This ensemble is linked by a picturesque cloistered courtyard with a well, old ploughshares, stone benches and plants. A sculpture group commemorates the priest Pedro Camps as well as the Menorcans who emigrated with him to North America in the 18th century, and founded the town of St Augustine.

Below: Hermitage door, Monte Toro
Bottom: Fornells from Monte Toro

The church and the hermitage are both consecrated to the Virgen de Toro, Our Lady of the Bull, who is worshipped as the island's patron saint. According to the legend, a wild bull led a group of monks to a cave where they discovered a statue of the madonna – the statue that today adorns the altar in the church. Despite this story, the name actually derives from the Arab word *al-thor*, which means 'main mountain'.

Map on pages 48–9

A NUN'S LIFE

It's hard to believe the nuns here are running a hermitage when one considers how amazingly busy it is every day of the week. A souvenir shop and a restaurant help keep them above water financially. The shop contains everything that is even slightly souvenir-like, from a colouring book all the way to a copy of the Christ statue, while the restaurant is a good place to sample *carquinyols* or *amargos* from Es Mercadal while enjoying the view across the Tramuntana and the Migjorn. If any of the provisions run out, one of the nuns drives down into the valley in an ancient Renault 4. During the summer this place is only ever really quiet in the early morning or evening, when the hordes of visitors have disappeared.

Below: statue of Christ, Monte Toro
Bottom: Ferreries street

FERRERIES

The fifth-largest town on the island, **Ferreries** (pop. 3,700), is also the highest. It lies at 142m (465ft) above sea-level, but is far less picturesque than Alaior. Even though the town centre, with its narrow streets, its Plaça de l'Església and parish church of **Sant Bartomeu**, is attractive, the scene is dominated by a large area of new housing with high apartment blocks and an industrial area.

Founded by Jaume II of Mallorca at the beginning of the 14th century, Ferreries consisted of

just a few houses and a village church until the 18th century, and was known mainly for its blacksmiths. After Governor Richard Kane decided to build the connecting road between Maó and Ciutadella the town prospered, and freed itself from dependence on Es Mercadal.

No-one is sure whether the name derives from *la fraria* (place of the monks) or *ferrería* (smithy), but the community today lives from a thriving furniture and shoe industry. The centre of action in Ferreries is the Plaça d'Espanya, where a large market is held every Saturday morning.

The best thing about Ferreries is that it makes a good starting-point for walks through the surrounding area. A variety of different landscapes converge here: the flat land in the west, the hilly north and the ravine-filled south.

PUIG DE SANTA AGUEDA

Just 3.5km (2 miles) outside Ferreries you will see a sign to the estate of **Binisues** on the right-hand side of the road. This is a stately home belonging to one of Ciutadella's noble families and is complete with the original furnishings. There is a museum of rural life here, as well as a pleasant restaurant with a big terrace, delicious wine and a great view.

There's another reason to come here: a walk to the summit of ★★ **Puig de Santa Agueda** (264m/ 866ft), the third-highest peak on the island but be sure to have good strong shoes or boots with you.

Leaving Binisues on your left, park your car at the old schoolhouse and take the footpath that leads up behind it to the right. The walk takes about half an hour; at first the steep path leads through a grove of cork oak and is difficult to negotiate because of rocks and stones. After 15 minutes or so, you will reach a remarkably well-preserved section of paved Roman path, evidence that the hill was already fortified in Roman times.

On the summit are the ruins of the **Castell de Santa Agueda**, an old Arab fort dating from the Moorish occupation. The governors of Medina Minurka had their summer palace here, and it was

Below: church of Sant Bartomeu
Bottom: Ferreries

Map
on pages
48–9

Ancient Quarry
Close to Torre Trencada, on the old road from Ciutadella to Maó, S'Hostal is a disused limestone quarry that has been turned into an unusual open-air museum. Workmen give demonstrations of quarrying techniques and you can walk right down into the quarry, beaneath the sheer limestone walls. It was from quarries such as this that the stone for Naveta d'es Tudons was probably extracted.

Torre Llafuda

the final Muslim stronghold to surrender after the Christian invasion. You can also make out the foundation walls of a chapel to St Agatha, as well as the ruins of a farmhouse that was in use until the 19th century. But the real rewards for taking this hike are the incomparable silence, broken only by the odd bleat of sheep, the rich vegetation, and a view of Menorca that is second to none.

PREHISTORIC SITES

The prehistoric village of **Torre Llafuda** was probably inhabited until Moorish times, and is hidden away to the left beneath mighty oak trees, amid a field of knee-high thistles. There are several ancient stones lying around, and the *talayot* here is thought to be the largest on Menorca. A surrounding wall full of passageways, and several Roman tracks nearby prove that the settlement was once of great importance to this region.

From here, Menorca's picture-postcard prehistoric site known as the ★ **Taula Torre Trencada** is only 1km (½ mile) away as the crow flies, but to reach it you have to get back to the C721, then turn left 2km (1 mile) further on (on the Camí Vell) and follow a bumpy asphalt track between high walls (keep left at the fork). The top stone of the *taula* (visible from afar and one of six similar structures that still survive on Menorca), is 3m (10ft) above the ground and supported by two other stones rather than just one – an unusual feature. The stone circle that belongs to it has survived the ravages of time, and there are several small funerary caves here too Although some of the stone slabs get used as picnic tables these days, the Torre Trencada is as captivating as ever.

NAVETA D'ES TUDONS

The fact that there is a route leading from the main road to the car park at the ★★★ **Naveta d'es Tudons** is significant, for this remarkable Bronze Age burial chamber standing in the middle of a field is the most famous prehistoric monument in Menorca. Since being excavated in the 1950s, it has become a magnet for visitors to the island, and features as an integral part of organised day trips here from Mallorca.

During the excavations, the remains of 50 people were discovered in this two-storey *naveta*, with its distinctive boat-like outline. Some were stored in quicklime and furnished with funerary ornaments of bronze. Despite the many finds, experts are still uncertain about the exact date of these *navetas* (derived from *navis*, the Latin word for a ship); theories vary from 2000BC to 1000BC. Be that as it may, the Naveta d'es Tudons is believed to be the oldest roofed building in Europe.

If you creep inside through the waist-high opening, you will see the two chambers above each other, separated by a ceiling made of stone slabs. A well-beaten path leads to a small rise – the best place for photographing this mysterious site, which looks quite magnificent in the early morning or evening light.

Star Attraction
• **Naveta d'es Tudons**

CATTLE SHEDS

The stepped pyramids that you pass on the way to Ciutadella are not relics of prehistory, but far more recent. The inventive Menorcans used the numerous stones in their fields to build artistic-looking cattle sheds known as *barraques*, a common feature of the western hinterland.

Naveta d'es Tudons

Map
on pages
48–9

4: The North

Maó – Albufera d'es Grau – Es Grau – Cap de Favaritx – Port d'Addaia – Fornells – Cap de Cavalleria – Es Mercadal (115km/71 miles)

Below: Albufera d'es Grau
Bottom: yachts and
windsurfers at Es Grau

The Tramuntana, the barren northern part of Menorca, is a rough landscape characterised by sharp rocky outcrops and smooth hills. It is more unspoilt and less touristy than the Migjorn in the south, although there are several modern tourist centres along its coast, such as Arenal d'en Castell. This region is good for hiking – and equally good for just stopping and staring.

The best of the scenery is along the coast: steep cliffs with lighthouses can be seen at Cap de Favaritx and Cap de Cavalleria. Between deep inlets there are protected sandy beaches and pretty little villages clinging to the slopes. The spiny lobster caught in Fornells is reputed to be the best in the western Mediterranean. If you want to hike, swim and eat superbly, plan to spend three days on this northern route.

ALBUFERA D'ES GRAU

The second-largest wet biotope in the Balearic Islands, ★★**S'Albufera d'es Grau**, is located north of Maó. Follow the PM710 towards Fornells, and after about 2km (1 mile) turn right along

the PMV7102, which twists its way through gently undulating landscape towards the coast for 10km (6 miles). In the 1970s, the biotope, centred on the only freshwater lake in Menorca, nearly had to make way for a new tourist development known as Shangri-La. Roads were built through the hilly landscape with its pine trees, street lamps were placed everywhere and the region – which is home to lizards, turtles, and all kinds of migratory birds – was parcelled up in preparation for the construction of a golf course, a swimming pool and numerous holiday homes.

Protests from the Menorcans, from environmental groups and from the WWF brought the project to a standstill. Roads leading to nowhere and several remote houses stand today as reminders of the failed construction project, and of the victory for the environmentalists. In May 1995, a year and a half after Menorca was designated a UNESCO-protected area – a Biosphere Reserve – the island government declared the 1,800-ha (4,450-acre) area a nature reserve.

Star Attraction
• **Albufera d'es Grau**

👁 **Birdwatchers' paradise**
Cormorants, herons, fish eagles and other species now live on the shores of the S'Albufera d'es Grau lagoon undisturbed, while human beings are only allowed to make brief visits here. Bird-watchers can hike along marked routes. It's best to bring along insect repellent, however, and check for ticks when you get back to your hotel in the evening.

ES GRAU

On the eastern edge of the reserve is the small, attractive fishing village of ★ **Es Grau**, which was founded by people from Maó at the beginning of the 20th century. The white houses are huddled close together and tlocal people still outnumber visitors, even though Es Grau is definitely a tourist centre these days. There are several pleasant bars, and the long semi-circular bay with its fishing boats and yachts is a picture-postcard scene.

The sand on the beach is fine and the water calm – making this place ideal for children. A surfboard hire centre is not far away, and there is at least one fisherman who offers trips to the uninhabited **Illa d'en Colom**, the Island of Pigeons. It's the largest of Menorca's offshore islands, and has two beaches and several ruins. The remains of a quarantine station date back to British rule here.

Beyond Es Grau is a broad view of the jagged cliffs and the lighthouse at Cap de Favaritx *(see page 64)*.

Es Grau beach

Map
on pages
48–9

Below: Ermita de Fátima
Bottom: Port d'Addaia

PICNIC SPOT

Back on the PM710 to Fornells, large, weathered-looking letters spell out *Lisa te quiero* (Lisa, I love you) on a cattle-shed wall, and the Camí d'en Kane *(see page 50)*, the old road between Maó and Ciutadella, branches off to the left. On the right of the PM710 you will see the **Ermita de Fátima** on a hilltop. There was a parish church on this site back in the Middle Ages, but today's structure dates from the 1950s. It's usually closed to visitors, but elderly people like sitting outside it at sunset and having picnic suppers.

CAP DE FAVARITX

The bumpy road to ★★ **Cap de Favaritx** crosses a barren, lunar landscape culminating in a headland lashed by the *tramuntana* wind. This region supports next to no vegetation apart from scrub and violet-coloured succulents in spring. On stormy days, the road looks decidedly dicy for the last few miles, almost as if the sea could make the crumbling grey slate cliffs collapse once and for all. That said, the cape has an eerie beauty.

At the end is the **Far de Favaritx**, the lighthouse, closed to visitors. Hardly any tourist buses make it as far as this remote corner of the island – usually just the odd angler or snorkeller. To the southeast, the two remote sandy beaches of **Cala Presili** and **Cala Tortuga** can be reached on foot from here in around half an hour.

PORT D'ADDAIA AND NA MACARET

Having returned from the cape, continue for around 1km (½ mile) along the PM710 to where an unmarked track leads off a bend to the right across fields to the **Ermita de Sant Llorenc de Binixems** *(see page 55)*. It can be reached from here on foot or by bike but not by car, because the route is too bumpy and the tree branches too low.

If you stay on the main road, however, and follow the signpost to Arenal d'en Castell, ★ **Port d'Addaia** is a worthwhile place to visit. This harbour lies at the end of a winding, fjord-like inlet that is best reached on foot. Villas, palm trees, oleanders, an old defensive tower dating from the years of British rule, converted into a summer residence, all make Addaia seem like a big, well-ordered park. The picturesquely situated Port Llum is a marina usually filled with yachts.

The little harbour town of **Na Macaret** owes its foundation in the 19th century to islanders who enjoyed fishing here in the summer and turned this place into a home from home. The same applies today: people from nearby towns enjoy sitting on the terraces of summer homes during the evening, admiring their boats rocking on the waves. Once autumn comes, the shutters are closed, the boats are placed in dry dock, and Na Macaret falls back into its winter sleep.

ARENAL D'EN CASTELL

The next stop, **Arenal d'en Castell**, is one of the few places on the island to have succumbed wholeheartedly to mass tourism, complete with two ugly hotels towering over the beach and a dense complex of holiday apartments. Although packed, the beach – a wide arc of golden sand – is perfect. Everything can be rented, from surfboards to sunshades, yachts and beach chairs. In the evening life can get very noisy with all the discos and clubs.

Star Attraction
• Cap de Favaritx

Natural harbour
Chosen by the British as the bridgehead for their final invasion of Menorca in 1798, the natural harbour at Port d'Addaia is noted for its excellent anchorage for yachts. The boatyard at the marina specialises in complete refits.

The popular Arenal d'en Castell

Map on pages 48–9

Travels on a donkey

For a leisurely ride through the Menorcan countryside, why not travel on a donkey? You can do this for a morning or afternoon from the Donkey Safari Park. Bear in mind, however, that the sacks used for saddles don't provide much of a cushion for bony backbones, and that the nags tend to go where they want rather than where you want them to go. Apart from the donkeys, there are lots of small animals for the children. There's also a small bar along with a café and shop, and the local people come here often to celebrate at the large barbecue sites, where they grill meat and eat it with *alioli*.

A patient donkey

DONKEY RIDES AND GOLF

Back on the PM710, oak trees grow to the very edge of the road, which sometimes appears to cut straight through the rock. A Donkey Safari Park comes into view in the forest on the left *(see box)*.

To the north of the main road, in the luxury urbanisation of **Son Parc**, tourism comes into its own again, centred this time around a 9-hole **golf course** which was opened in 1977, and is still the only place on Menorca where the sport can be played. The course is pleasantly situated among pine groves.

FORNELLS

The fact that King Juan Carlos and his family have been to ★★ **Fornells** (pop. 650) on several occasions to eat *caldereta de langosta* is certainly worth a mention. This delicious lobster dish *(see page 105)* isn't the only reason to visit this pretty town, however, because Fornells, a gentle oasis along the rough north coast, has most of the ingredients one likes to imagine in a Mediterranean town: narrow streets lined with white, wooden-shuttered houses, a palm-fringed promenade along the calm lagoon, and colourful fishing boats side by side with yachts in the harbour basin. Visitors can hire surfboards, small boats, speedboats and enormous yachts, or get taken by a fisherman to visit the cavern known as the **Cova des Ingleses** (English Cove), the roof of which resembles the vault of a high church, with reddish-brown walls reflected in the azure water.

FORTS AND BEACHES

Anyone who prefers staying on land can hike to the **Torre de Fornells** (Tues–Sat 11am–2pm, 6–9pm, Sun 11am–2pm; free on Sun), built on the headland by the British in 1802. On the way there, at the water's edge, are the ruins of **Sant Antoni**, the 17th-century fortress that protected the little fishing village until it was destroyed by the Spanish in 1782. In the evening people either meet up in the parish church of Sant Antoni or on the

long harbour jetty to watch the sunset, before heading for one of the numerous restaurants and trying a *caldereta* or some other fishy dish.

The best way to get to Fornells' local beach of **Cala Tirant** is to drive or to walk along a path that runs the length of the rocky coast. It takes nearly four hours if you go on foot, but the fine bay with its broad sandy beach makes it well worth the effort. On its western edge lies the holiday village of the same name, and to the east is the **Platjes de Fornells** 'country club' with large parks and white, estate-style houses. Palm-trees and agaves along the narrow streets complete the picture and the view stretches for miles.

Star Attraction
• Fornells

CAVALLERIA

The region to the west of Fornells is known as Cavalleria, after the Cavalleries – the local estates built for military reasons after the *reconquista*. The whole area has been declared an area of special interest, not only because of the outstanding countryside, but also because of the number of archaeological remains that have been discovered here. To the left and right of the road leading west there are fields of daisies and wild fennel. Anyone interested in bird-life can make discoveries right at the roadside: birds of prey such as buzzards can be seen circling, and herons stalk

Below: Torre de Fornells
Bottom: Fornells harbour wall

Map on pages 48–9

👁 **Walk on the wild side**
If you feel like getting more than just a fleeting impression of the rugged country in the north, leave your car near the Alairó farm and walk along one of the hiking paths westwards. There are a few olive groves, vegetable plots, and the odd farm – otherwise the region is characterised by wild vegetation and reddish-coloured rocks. At some point the north side of the Puig de Santa Agueda *(see page 59)* comes into view, and the paths keep on ending at closed gates bearing the message 'Propriedad Privada – Prohibido el Paso' so that in the end one has to obey them and set off back.

Feeding the goats

the marshland. Soon the surface starts getting rough and stony and a dusty track leads northwards, just passing the fine sandy beach **Platja de Cavalleria** and the remote **Cala Mica** beach; if you feel like a swim at this point, keep left.

Further north still, the track passes a bright, white farmhouse called Sa Cavalleria, with a square defensive tower. The shallow bay near the **Torre de Sanitja**, constructed by the British in 1798, was the third most important harbour on the island during Roman times. Today it just contains the odd fishing boat. The remains of the Roman settlement of **Sanitja** have only recently been discovered by archaeologists. Excavations are not finished yet and each year from June to October you will find further attempts to discover more.

CAP DE CAVALLERIA

This area is totally deserted. With a bit of luck, you may spot a rare type of vulture known as a *moixeta (Neophron percnopterus)*. There are numerous gates along the way until finally the ★★ **Cap de Cavalleria**, Menorca's and also the Balearic Islands' northernmost point, comes into view. Offshore is the tiny Illa des Porros. The steep coast reaches the imposing height of 89m (290ft) here at the Cap, on the top of which is the **Far de Cavalleria**, protected from outsiders by a wall. All around it are caves dug during the Spanish Civil War, but today they are populated exclusively by lizards. It's best not to venture in too far because of the danger that they may collapse.

There's no alternative now but to go back along the same bumpy route. To the west of Sa Cavalleria farm is the beach of **Binimel-là**, an excellent place for a swim. In high season there's also a *xiringuito*, or beach bar, that sells *tapas*. A path leads over hills, stone walls and sand dunes to **Cala Pregonda**, a pretty bay with a small beach that is hardly ever busy even in high summer. Hikers can venture even further to Cala Barrll (three hours there and back), a long valley and shady pine forest have to be crossed before the tiny bay comes into view behind a hillcrest.

5: The Southeast

Maó – Sant Lluis – Cala d'Alcaufar – Punta Prima – Binibeca Vell – Es Canutells – Cales Coves – Torralba d'en Salort – Alaior (69km/42 miles)

Map on pages 48–9

Star Attraction
• Cap de Cavalleria

The southeast of Menorca has some attractive beaches, and sports centres make all kinds of watersports possible. The tourist settlements vary in quality: the colours and dimensions of the most recently built ones harmonise best with the landscape. A good example of successful architecture is the unusual holiday village of Poblat de Pescadores near Binibeca Vell. Towns such as Sant Lluís are good places to go for a meal, then to discover properly while wandering and window-shopping later on.

Below: a local shopkeeper
Bottom: Playa Punta Prima

ANCIENT SITES

The south of the island is also a good place for adventurers, however, as a glance at the *Mapa Arqueológico de Menorca* (available in local bookshops) will show: the region has a concentration of prehistoric sites, especially the *talayots* of Torrellonet and So Na Cacana, as well as the settlement of Torralba d'en Salort. In the Cales Coves – over 100 caves dug out of the rock – a 3,000-year-old culture can be examined *(see page 75)*. The Cova d'en Xoroi in the steep coastal

Map on pages 48–9

Watersports
For watersports along this flat, rocky coast the best address is the Club S'Algar Diving & Watersports. All kinds of sports are available, from windsurfing and sailing to water-skiing and jet-skiing – and divers are provided for too. Underwater caves, coral reefs and bays are visited during diving trips, and booking ahead in good time ensures a place on the boat.

Sant Lluís windmill

rocks is quite different – it's a cave disco, and the thumping bass tones resonate out across the sea until the early hours of the morning. Plan roughly two and a half days for this route.

SANT LLUIS

Take the road from Maó to **Sant Lluís** (pop. 3,100), which is pleasant but unspectacular: its narrow, quiet side-streets are grouped around the main Carrer de Sant Lluís. The park is as large as a football pitch and is filled with pine trees and climbing frames. In the **Centro Cultural** most of the older people tend to be engrossed in games of dominoes. The cups around the walls commemorate island football games.

Sant Lluís dates back to the French occupation of the island who founded the town during their seven-year stay. In accordance with the vision of the French governor of that time, the streets are arranged geometrically. The flat, white houses here are dominated by the neo-classical **parish church**, built in 1762 and consecrated to the canonised Louis IX; and the **Molí de Dalt** (May–Oct, Wed–Mon 10am–1pm, 7–9pm; Nov–Apr, Mon, Wed–Sat 9am–2pm), a lovingly restored windmill housing a small folk museum with a collection of traditional farm tools.

S'ALGAR

Take a left turn at the distinctive, dove-decorated roundabout on the edge of town, towards **S'Algar**, one of the first holiday resorts on Menorca. It gives one an idea of what the tourist areas in the south of the island are like: white, elegant apartments in long rows, broken up by palm trees and pines. Supermarkets here, car rental services there, plus a few restaurants and a discotheque – everything is catered for. Away from the water *(see box)* the days can be spent playing tennis, cricket, bowling, or horse-riding from the Club Hipic es Boeret.

A restored section of the coastal bridleway, Camí de Cavalls – which once ran around the entire Menorcan coast *(see page 11)* – connects S'Algar with Cala d'Alcaufar just to the south and onwards to the **Platja de Punta Prima** *(see below)*. It takes about two and a half hours there and back without a break, and remember that the sun beats down most of the time.

To the north of S'Algar a narrow footpath leads to the peaceful **Barranc de Rafalet**. Hikers should manage to get there and back in one and a half hours. After crossing a few fields and scaling several walls, the route descends into the valley and the fjord-like bay is reached at the end of an oak grove. The rocky outcrops here are often photographed to advertise Menorcan holidays.

Punta Prima shopping and beach

CALA D'ALCAUFAR AND PUNTA PRIMA

A high embankment, a long bay and a little sandy beach are the special features of ★ **Cala d'Alcaufar**. The settlement has also retained something that other towns on the south coast lost long ago: the atmosphere of a fishing village. Low, white houses with wooden balconies and boat-houses with blue or green gates are the picturesque backdrop . While tourists lie on the beach, the fishermen mend their nets or paint their boats nearby.

One of the oldest holiday resorts on Menorca is **Punta Prima**, and it is highly regarded because

Map on pages 48–9

Shipwrecks
The southernmost cape of Menorca around Punta Prima is not without its share of dangers, as can be inferred from the *Nautical Guide Menorca*, published in Maó: there are plenty of shipwrecks just under the waterline along this stretch of coast.

of its broad, sandy beach. As a result, the hotels and apartments do a busy trade in summer time, as do those who rent sunbeds by the water's edge. The outlets advertising surfboard hire have plenty of customers, too, and when the wind blows in from the sea there are numerous surfers out on the waves. Divers favour the coastline of the nearby **Illa de l'Aire**, with its tall lighthouse.

A STRING OF RESORTS

The section of coast to the west contains one *urbanización* after the next: Biniancolla is followed by Cala Torret, then Binibeca Vell, and finally Binissafúller and Binidalí. Most of these holiday complexes have features in common: one is the Arabic origin of the place names with the prefix *Bini*, which means 'property of the sons of...'. The other is the tiny beaches on sheltered bays, with just a few traces remaining of the fishing communities they once used to be.

The newly-built coast road, illuminated in the evenings by a row of modern street lamps, is ideal for making quick progress. Whenever it stops, as it sometimes does, the best rule of thumb is to follow the one-way systems until another side-street heads towards the sea again – otherwise you may end up in a dead end in one of the interminable holiday complexes.

Imaginative architecture at Binibeca Vell

BINIBECA VELL

An exception to most of the holiday villages in this part of Menorca is ★★★ **Binibeca Vell** (also spelled Binibequer Vell). In 1972, when large high-rise hotels were being favoured in other areas, the tourist village of Poblat de Pescadors was built around this little settlement in traditional Menorcan style. The plans were drawn up by Spanish architect, Antonio Sintes – a man with vision – who has been awarded many prizes.

Star Attraction
• Binibeca Vell

The houses, washed in brilliant white, look as if they are made of icing sugar. Stairs, chimneys and balconies are all completely harmonious. Narrow, winding alleys emerge into small interior courtyards, finished with natural stone and decorated with ceramic tiles; there are palms and orange trees at every corner, and bougainvillaea tumbles over garden walls. Bars and restaurants, a market place, a church and quay have also been constructed as an integral part of the settlement.

The overall effect is beautiful, but strangely unreal and the hordes of visitors dropped off by tour coaches during the summer months add to the impression that this is part of a film set.

Below: Binibeca Vell detail
Bottom: Es Canutells bay

ES CANUTELLS

Beyond Binidalí the coast road comes to an end, and another runs inland through beautiful landscape towards the centre of the island, past lush green fields, farms and a riding stable, until there's a left turn towards ★ **Es Canutells** and the sea again. This bay is beautiful, and surrounded protectively by rocks; the community here is small, as is the white sandy beach, and things remain calm and peaceful here in the summertime. Fishing boats filled with lobster pots dock at the quay, and elderly local people chat away outside their summer residences.

PREHISTORIC CAVES

The housing area of Ses Tanques is half an hour's walk to the east. Beneath it, along the imposingly steep coast, there are numerous ★ **prehistoric**

Map on pages 48–9

caves. Only try exploring them if you have a head for heights. Some caves contain several chambers and others have supports shoring them up – all have dizzying views of the sea below. The best view of all can be had from the rocky headland opposite, on which a British fort once stood.

SAN CLIMENT

The little village of **Sant Climent** is popular with residents of Maó. People who live in the 'Binis' stop at Carrer de Sant Jaume and buy all they need for the day, but don't spend much more time here. There's a little plaça and a parish church, a pub advertising 'Friday night knockout darts', a jazz club with good music and a *pastelería* with delicious *pastas* and *rosquillas* – and that just about sums up Sant Climent.

Below: Sant Climent jazz club holds jazz nights every Tuesday and Thursday
Bottom: Talayot de Torrellonet

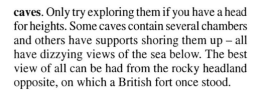

TORRELONET

After all this indolent beach life, you shouldn't lose sight of the island's prehistory. There's a good detour to the northeast at this point to the highest surviving *talayot* on Menorca, the **Torrellonet**. As you open and close the numerous gates on the way there, you will hear charter jets taking off and landing nearby. The Torrellonet is the only *talayot* on the island which has a window, but

rather disrespectfully it has been equipped with flight tracking equipment for the airport. The steps leading up were worn away long ago – but there's a good view, as you would expect from a defensive tower.

If you continue along the path for around 500m (¼ mile), past a farm with some moody dogs, you'll catch sight of the **Basílica d'es Fornàs**. This early Christian church, built in the 5th or 6th century, is located above the foundations of a Roman villa. The remains of the three aisles and a filigree floor mosaic with peacocks, lions and foliage survive. The whole structure has been roofed over, and barbed wire protects it from unauthorised entry.

Along the road westwards to Sant Climent there are more, smaller *talayots* and also the excellent English-run Rancho Allenwood, which organises riding lessons as well as whole day rides with picnics included *(see page 110)*.

Star Attraction
•**Cales Coves**

> **Communal living**
> In Talyotic times, the caves of Cales Coves were used both as burial chambers and as dwellings, with the dead and the living housed in adjacent caves. The more modern caves, dating from the 4th century BC, are quite sophisticated in design, with windows, patios and separate cubicles for different family members.

CALES COVES

Reaching the ★★ **Cales Coves** (Cave Bays), requires some tough driving in a hire car or an hour's hike, but it's worth the trip: the two bays with their high limestone walls and numerous prehistoric caves, several of which are on different levels, are among the most impressive sights along the south coast.

This double bay has been a popular harbour since antiquity. The first caves were dug here in around 1000BC, and by the 4th century AD there were around 100 of them. They were used later on as hiding places by pirates and fishermen, and today a small group of dropouts lives here.

In the summer time so many young backpackers are attracted here from all over Europe that hardly a free cave can be found. The municipal authorities in Alaior make regular attempts to evict people from this free accommodation, but the holes – which have been declared a Spanish national monument – are soon reoccupied, and adherents of natural living return to splash about in the picturesque bays.

The Cales Coves

Map
on pages
48–9

👁 **Cova d'en Xoroi**
According to legend this cave was once inhabited by a pirate named Xoroi, 'the one-eared'. He stole from the farmers in the region, eventually abducting a farmer's daughter and fathering three sons by her. His hiding place was discovered shortly afterwards, whereupon Xoroi jumped into the sea with his eldest son.

Below: Torralba d'en Salort
Bottom: Cova d'en Xoroi

CALA EN PORTER

Not far away, **Cala en Porter** is tourist country again, and has a surfeit of apartments, restaurants, bars, discos, hotels, supermarkets and estate agencies eager to sell people second homes. The long sandy beach with high cliffs can be reached by a flight of steps cut into the limestone, or by car.

One highlight here is the ★ **Cova d'en Xoroi**, a cave disco set into the steep coast. It is 25m (82ft) above the waterline, set between sea and sky. In the afternoon, tourists can sit in a café here and sip their tea while they admire the scenery; in the evening, pop music thunders out of the cave, accompanied by light shows.

TORRALBA D'EN SALORT

Along the road to Alaior with its many bends, are three prehistoric sites: first, on the left, are the almost-overgrown remains of the village of So Na Cacana, with two *talayots*. Another 800m (½ mile) further along the road you must turn left yet again to reach ★ **Torre Llisá Vell** (park at the first farm, then keep left and go past several walls). Its entrance area – an archway and walls 3m (10ft) thick – is the only intact one of a Menorcan *taula*.

The prehistoric settlement of ★★ **Torralba d'en Salort** (Oct–May, Mon–Sat 10am–1pm, 3–6pm; Jun–Sept, daily 10am–8pm), one of the few to open at specific hours and charge admission fees, features remarkable building methods – the rocks were piled on top of each other long before the invention of the pulley. In around 900BC this settlement was one of the largest on Menorca, as can be seen from the imposing *taula*, two *talayots*, numerous ruined houses and caves. Two hearths were discovered near the *taula* during excavation work, and are thought to have served as altars for ritual animal sacrifices. A small bronze bull and fragments of a bronze figurine were also found, and they are now on display in the Museu de Menorca (*see page 29*). A few years ago the Fundació de les Illes Baleares (Balearic Islands Foundation) purchased the entire site, and it became the first archaeological park on the island.

6: The Rocky South

Alaior – Torre d'en Gaumés – Platja de Son Bou – Es Migjorn Gran – Cova d'es Coloms – Sant Agustí Vell – Cala Santa Galdana – Barranc d'Algendar (60km/37 miles)

The Migjorn, the southern central part of Menorca, is packed with ancient watchtowers and those massive stone tablets that make Menorca one enormous outdoor prehistoric museum. For some people the sites are places of pilgrimage, while others steer clear of them; some like meditating here while others see nothing but a meaningless heap of old rocks. The Menorcans swear that whoever touches a *taula* during the full moon will have good luck and true love for the rest of their life – so that's a good enough reason to visit a few of them.

WORLDS APART

The landscape in the south of Menorca is more gentle than that in the north, and there's more tourist development here too. The local inhabitants are said to be different as well – more warm and friendly than their northern compatriots. Near the sea there are several pine groves plus innumerable holiday apartment complexes. The powerful sunshine here in the south can get very hot

Map on pages 48–9

Star Attraction
• Torralba d'en Salort

Son Bou beach is great for families

Map
on pages
48–9

👁 **Archaeological finds**
Finds unearthed at Torre
d'en Galmés include
Phoenician ceramics and Roman
coins as well as a bronze statue of
the Egyptian god Imhotep.

at times, providing a good excuse to seek shade
during a day trip to the *barrancs* – deep gorges.
The Barranc d'Algendar, for instance, has a tropical climate and vegetation to match. This route
should take two to three days to complete, and
four if you go on the hikes as well.

TORRE D'EN GALMÉS

The biggest megalithic settlement on Menorca,
★★ **Torre d'en Galmés** (Tues–Sun 10am–2pm,
5–8pm) was discovered to the south of Alaior during the 1940s, but only properly excavated in the
1960s. More than 500 people are thought to have
lived here as long ago as 1000BC, and the settlement was robably the island's capital because
it has three *talayots*, a temple area with a *taula*,
long defensive walls, caves and cisterns. The oldest part of the site comprises the tomb chambers
and a pillared hall covered by stone slabs – probably a place of assembly.

A small road leads around the entire archaeological site, leading some visitors simply to peer
at it from their car windows – but that means they
miss the important sights. This town, inhabited
until the Middle Ages by the Menorcans' fore-
fathers, is like one enormous stone garden, full of
flowers and lizards – and the view extends as far
as Alaior and Monte Toro.

Torre d'en Galmés

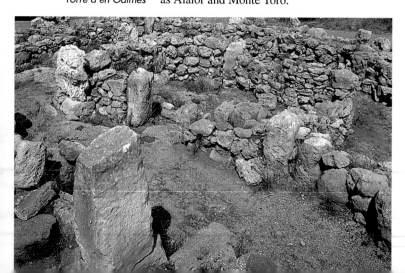

CAP DE SE PENYES

Further on towards the coast, a narrow side-road, paved at first, leads to the 70-m (230-ft) high **Cap de se Penyes**. The best thing to do is park at the beginning of the route and continue on foot, so as to enjoy the view across the beach of Son Bou and the Basílica Paleocristina, with the Cap d'Artrutx far away in the distance. On its eastern side the cape is bordered by the jagged Barranc de Llucalari, one of the rough valleys in the south. To reach the fine sandy beach at the end of the *barranc* you should take one of the narrow paths further inland.

EARLY CHRISTIAN BASILICA

The remains of a 5th-century Early Christian structure, the **Basílica Paleocristina**, lie to the east of Son Bou, near the beach – which means that many of its visitors are clad in swimming trunks or bikinis. Its walls were discovered in 1951, and it is assumed that the basilica once formed part of a larger settlement, the streets of which can still be made out from aerial photographs of the surrounding area.

The basilica originally had three aisles, and seems to have been influenced by similar structures in North Africa. One highlight of the site is a monolithic font in the form of a clover leaf. In the nearby section of steep coastline, Menorcans of an even earlier age created a striking cave community. Several of their descendants have converted the caves into holiday residences.

PLATJA DE SON BOU

When you see the long, fine sandy **Platja de Son Bou**, sloping smoothly into the water and perfect for children, it becomes clear why the adjoining residential developments of Son Bou and Torre Soli Nou, as well as the villa community of Sant Jaume, are grouped around it like a miniature amphitheatre. This panorama close to the beach attracted the attention of tourism developers very early on. Several 11-storey hotel blocks date from

Star Attraction
• **Torre d'en Gaumés**

Below: Son Bou basilica
Bottom: the beach

Map
on pages
48–9

Arts and crafts

Art fans visiting Es Migjorn Gran can drop in at the Galeria Migjorn Graham Byfield in the Carrer San Llorec to admire and perhaps purchase the ceramics and watercolours produced by much-travelled English artist Graham Byfield, with motifs from all over the world, as well as the naïve paintings of Peri Rowan (Tues–Sat 10am–1pm and 6–9pm, closed January to April).

the unplanned construction boom in the 1960s, while today's buildings have been limited to four storeys in height. Son Bou only comes to life in the holiday season – during the winter the area beyond the dunes is like one enormous ghost town.

Between the dunes and the built-up part of the coastline is the largest area of marshland in the southern part of the island, **Es Prat de Son Bou**. It was thanks to the efforts of the environmentalist group, Grup Ornitológic Balear (GOB) that the marshland was not drained to produce more land for construction. The area has now been declared a nature reserve, and during a stroll through it you may be lucky enough to catch a glimpse of a kite, a falcon or similar species of bird.

ES MIGJORN GRAN

Hardly anything has changed in the small town of ★ **Es Migjorn Gran** since it was founded in the second half of the 18th century. This was the home of the doctor Francesc Camps, who was also an amateur archaeologist and Menorca expert; he documented numerous songs and local customs. The town's name changed from Sant Cristòfol to Es Migjorn Gran when it became part of the municipality of Es Mercadal in 1990. Es Migjorn Gran means 'the big south', and Menorcans have actually referred to the town by that

Es Migjorn cemetery

name since time immemorial. The name San Cristobal – which was given to the town and its 18th-century parish church by the Spanish – can still be seen on some maps of the island.

GOURMET CENTRE

As the only one of Menorca's municipalities that does not lie on the main road, Es Migjorn Gran has a sleepy, provincial feel and lots of traditional rural architecture. The simple whitewashed houses along Carrer Major, none of which is more than two storeys, have balconies and wooden shutters, and some are decorated with blue tiles. The parish church of Sant Cristòfol, its square bell-tower topped by a cockerel, is satisfyingly proportioned. This little town has made a name for itself as a gourmet food centre over the past few years for its traditional Menorcan restaurants, such as S'Engolidor or Migjorn *(see page xxx)*.

BARRANC DE BINIGAUS

Not far from Es Migjorn Gran, several *barrancs* lead down to the sea. One of the strangest and wildest looking is the **Barranc de Binigaus**, which culminates at the beach of Binigaus to the west of Sant Tomás. The hiking route there begins at the peaceful old cemetery, and passes three *talayots* as well as several fields full of pigs and cows. A path that is easy to miss (look for the red arrow on the wall) leads down into the narrow ravine, and alongside the usually dry river-bed below. Plants such as foxgloves flourish in the humid micro-climate on the valley floor, among liana-covered oak, almond and olive trees.

COVA D'ES COLOMS

If you look carefully on the opposite side of the ravine you will find the hidden entrance to the ★ **Cova d'es Coloms**, a cave known locally as 'the cathedral', and not without reason. Its dimensions are gigantic, though estimates of how big it actually is tend to vary wildly. Anyone who comes

Below: inside Es Migjorn church
Bottom: melon picking

Map on pages 48–9

Below: Cova d'es Coloms
Bottom: a talayot

here and tries to guess will soon realise that the rear section of the cave is concealed in the darkness. If you try to throw a stone at the ceiling, it won't get there.

Excavations here have revealed numerous cult objects from pre-Christian times, when the ravines on the island were densely populated and the caves served as cult centres. Traces of campfires and graffiti on the walls are of a far more recent date, however. Young people like to have parties down here, dragging along generators for their amplifiers, guitars and microphones, as well as bringing all the necessary supplies of alcohol and food for barbecuing.

SANT AGUSTI VELL

At the entrance to the cave, an almost invisible stony path leads out of the ravine again. At the top on the right you will arrive at the prehistoric settlement of ★★ **Sant Agustí Vell**, which can also be reached by car if you park on the main road from Es Migjorn Gran to San Tomás opposite the Son Saura estate and then walk down.

The village's picturesque location at the steep entrance to the *barranc* makes it clear that even the earliest Menorcans knew the benefits of a good view. Visitors today like settling down for picnics here, too. The settlement consists of the

remains of temples, houses, walls, cisterns and storage chambers set in the rock, covered with stone slabs and known as *sitjots*. One of the two remarkably well-preserved *talayots* here can be entered. Once your eyes have grown accustomed to the darkness, you will see three supporting pillars and a kind of stone crossbeam holding up the ceiling.

Star Attraction
•Sant Agustí Vell

SANT TOMÁS

The small collection of hotels and apartment villages known as **Sant Tomás** is worth visiting mostly for its flat, sandy beaches of Sant Adeodat and Sant Tomás. They're packed of course, because families with children adore the place. Even the apartments close to the sea have swimming pools, in case the guests are scared of the Mediterranean. The watersports provided here are very varied, and the beach bar of Es Bruc, with a large terrace facing the sea, is rather like an observation platform, providing its guests with a view of beach life from above.

Peaceful alternative
If you prefer things a bit quieter than the bustle of Sant Tomás, take your sun-mat and walk along the 1.5-km (1-mile) path leading to the quieter beach of Binigaus, further to the west. If you walk westwards and stay close to the shore you'll also reach the beach of Son Bou around 40 minutes later.

SON MERCER

The journey along the road from Es Migjorn Gran to Ferreries is like a roller-coaster ride. The road cuts deeply through the rock, leads past remote farms and attractive country estates, and takes you through green hills with small fields of corn and potatoes. Almost 1km (½ mile) before Ferreries a rough track winds up the slope to the left and is a good starting-point for a hike.

Once you reach the top there's a good view of Ferreries, and if you follow the path further you'll reach one of the very best views of the southern part of the island – the white limestone plateau, and numerous hills and *barrancs*.

Roughly 600m (⅓ mile) beyond the farm of Son Mercer de Baix is the village of ★ **Son Mercer de Baix**, which tourists hardly ever reach. This is a pity, because the prehistoric settlement is one of the oldest on the island: people settled in this unique location on the edge of the Barranc de Trebaluger

Outside in Sant Tomás

Map
on pages
48–9

and the Barranc de Son Fideu around 4,000 years ago. Excavations have also revealed pottery shards dating from Phoenician and Roman times. The foundations of several houses resembling *navetas* have been discovered beneath olive trees, including the **Cova d'es Moro**, or Moor's Cave, which has been a listed monument since 1931. The name is rather confusing because the cave is actually a well-preserved house with a roof supported by three stone pillars.

Below: Cala Santa Galdana
Bottom: an alternative view

CALA SANTA GALDANA

Another attractive route runs from Ferreries towards Menorca's most famous bay, the Cala Santa Galdana. Just 1km (½ mile) outside Ferreries is the **Club Escola Menorquina**, where spectacular horse shows are held on summer evenings (Jul–Sept, Wed and Sun, 8.30pm; tel: 971 15 50 59). The road then leads past Talaiot Binicalsitx and one of the two official campsites on the island *(see page 116)* before arriving at the bay of ★ **Cala Santa Galdana**. For a superb view of the natural scenery here, walk to the end of the rocky promontory to the left of the path: rocks fall steeply down to the sea; islands and peninsulas can be seen offshore; and pine forests and ravines extend as far as the semi-circular beach.

QUEEN OF THE COVES

A perfect oyster-shell bay, Cala Santa Galdana, known as the 'queen of the coves', is one of the finest in all the Balearic Islands. In the early 1960s it was overrun by mass tourism: there are three huge, high-rise hotels with room for 2,200 guests. The restaurants, bars, apartment villages and supermarkets arrived later, and in the summer the sandy beach is almost always full. Children splash about in the shallow water or race around in electric cars on a special track, while their parents laze under sunshades that stand in long lines. Surfing, sailing, snorkelling and diving are all provided. The astonishing thing is that despite all of this, the bay has managed to retain its beauty.

CALA MITJANETA AND CALA TREBALUGA

Anyone who wants to escape the summer crush can take a half-hour walk eastwards to the **Cala Mitjaneta**, and a little further on to the neighbouring bay of **Cala Trebaluga** (look for the red signposts from the Mitjaneta bay onwards). It takes a little longer to reach Cala Macarella and the smaller Cala Macarelleta further the west *(see page 88).* Experienced hikers can reach the Cap D'Artrutx from here in around five hours. Be sure to wear sturdy shoes, and stay close to the coast so you don't lose your bearings.

BARRANC D'ALGENDAR

If you follow the narrow course of the Torrent d'Algendar, which comes out in the Santa Galdana, the ★★**Barranc d'Algendar** ravine can't be missed. After you've bravely crossed a few typical Menorcan stiles with the message *Proprieda Privada,* you'll see a very unusual side of Menorca, at least if it's high summer.

The colours are quite different suddenly, and a broad valley turns into a *barranc* and then a true ravine a few miles further on, with sheer, 80-m (260-ft) high rocky walls. At first there are reeds on the banks of the river, and a scattering of wild fruit trees. But the narrower the ravine becomes, the more jungle-like the vegetation.

Star Attraction
• Barranc d'Algendar

Wild orchids
Wild orchids are no rarity in the Barranc d'Algendar, and butterflies will be your permanent companion until dusk forces you to make your way back again.

Snorkelling in the clear waters

Map
on page
93

👁 **Sun, sea and sand**
Don't expect any architectural gems here – but as recompense you'll get a broad range of entertainment that starts at dawn and goes on late into the night. The prehistoric settlement of Son Catlar, one of the largest and most interesting on the island, provides a respite from sea and sand.

7: Beaches of the Southwest

Ermita de Sant Joan de Missa – Cala en Turqueta – Cala Macarella – Son Catlar – Son Saura – Cala Santandría – Cap D'Artrutx – Ciutadella (66km/41 miles)

The dream beaches of Menorca are located to the southeast of Ciutadella, and the locals refer to them vividly as *platjes verges*, virgin beaches – with white sand, azure water and picturesquely framed by rocks. Shade is provided by pine groves along the coast and the cave bars on some beaches are like civilised additions. In this part of the island, construction projects of all kind have been successfully nipped in the bud. For instance, protests from Menorcans in the early 1990s managed to stop Cala Macarella being turned into a holiday enclave. The southwest coast, where the beaches are no less attractive, is a different story entirely: Cala Santandría or Cala Blanca are well-established resorts, and construction work at Cap d'Artrutx continues unabated.

If you want to indulge in lazy beach life and do the hikes, it's best to allow two days for this route.

ERMITA DE SANT JOAN DE MISSA

Ermita de Sant Joan de Missa

Along the road to Cala en Turqueta there are signs saying *Coto Privado de Caza* (private hunting land) every few metres, starting from the Plaça Jaume II in Ciutadella. Walls overgrown with capers line the narrow road that leads to the bays of the southwest; beyond them lie hidden gardens, barren, stony fields and a few farms. Always keep left wherever you reach a fork in the road.

Just away from the main road is the **Ermita de Sant Joan de Missa**, a small chapel with battlements that was built in 1634. A previous building on the site was mentioned in the island annals of 1330. From the square in front of today's church there is a broad view of southwestern Menorca all the way to the mountains of Mallorca in the distance. The little chapel itself is closed for most of the year. One way of making sure you gain access to it is to come here on the Festes de

Sant Joan, on 23 June, when a procession of riders arrives here from Ciutadella as part of the celebrations. Beyond the chapel to the left, an easily missed country track branches off to the left and to the pine-lined Cala Macarella, but it's in poor condition. If you do want to go to the fine sandy beach and don't mind an hour's walk, carry on driving straight ahead and you can reach it via the old Camí de Cavalls *(see page 11).*

Star Attraction
•**Cala en Turqueta**

MOTH TRAPS

Beyond the old country estate of Sant Francesc, a clay path leads down to the sea through a thick forest of oak and pine. Many of the pine trees have plastic boxes hanging from them – traps for tip moths which are renowned pine-tree killers throughout the Mediterranean. The females' propagation hormone emanates from the boxes, attracting the male moths, in an attempt to stop them from multiplying so rapidly. If nothing were done, just a few nests in one tree would be enough to destroy it in a few years' time.

*Two views of
Cala en Turqueta*

CALA EN TURQUETA

The shallow ★★ **Cala en Turqueta**, with its magnificent sandy beach, is perfect for families with children. The locals have turned several of the

Map
on page
93

Early warning
Watchtowers, such as the tower of Artrutx, were originally built to provide early warning of Ottoman fleets or pirate ships. Known as *atalayas*, they communicated with each other using light signals, and Monte Toro *(see page 56)* was the control centre.

caves here into formidable second residences – complete with projecting roofs made of reeds, pretty terraces and lots of palm trees. A small beach bar opens in one of the grottos here during the summer months, selling *tapas* for those feeling peckish.

High on a hill above the bay is the watchtower **Talaia d'Artrutx**, built in 1588. It is one of the best preserved of many such towers along the Menorcan coast, and the view from the top across the southern part of the island is excellent.

CALA D'ES TALAIER

To the west, not far from the Cala de Turqueta, is the ★ **Cala d'es Talaier**, or Guardians' Bay – perhaps the people in charge of the watchtower couldn't resist a quick dip in this bay in former times. The way eastwards is one of the nicest sections of the Camí de Cavalls *(see page 11)*, with aromatic pines, mastic trees and wild fig trees – with the sea in the background all the way.

First the path leads to ★ **Cala Macarelleta**, home to nudists and young backpackers with sleeping-bags during the summer; then on to the larger ★ **Cala Macarella**, which takes about an hour to reach. A few years ago it was considered an insider tip and today is popular with those eager to flee the bustle of Santa Galdana. Flanked by high rocks, this bay can also be reached on foot through pine woods from Cala Santa Galdana in around 30 to 40 minutes. The sand is fine, and a small bar provides refreshments.

To reach the beach of **Son Saura**, drive back to the first fork in the road beyond the Ermita de Sant Joan de Missa and then turn right down the road towards the sea. On the way you will pass the almost-invisible megalithic village of **Egipte**, the *talayots* of which have long since disappeared beneath the undergrowth.

*Beach football,
Cala Macarella*

SON CATLAR

Without a doubt, the highlight of this route is the prehistoric village of ★★★ **Son Catlar**, one of the finest on the Balearic Islands. The settlement is encircled by an 870-m (2,850-ft) wall, several metres thick, with the remains of square defensive towers and galleries and a gateway, and it was probably used most in the 3rd and 2nd centuries BC. Its origins date back to the Bronze Age, and the village was inhabited until the fall of the Roman Empire.

Within the well-preserved enclosing walls, five *talayots* and the *taula* can be made out. The coping stone on the central sanctuary caved in at some point and cracked. One of the special features of this site is the *hypogaeum*, a small underground chamber that was used for funerary purposes. The whole site is surrounded by oak, gorse and macchia, and sheep graze peacefully nearby; the view of the sea is excellent. Since the mid-1990s Son Catlar has been a UNESCO site, and there are explanatory signboards in four languages all over the place. There is also a small museum and restaurant. The sign on the first gate leading to the estate of Torre Saura, owned by Count Saura, reads: 'You enter private property, please respect the environment and use the obligated parking place.' The house itself cannot be visited, and the battlements on the tower that stands beside it can merely be admired from afar. As the route continues there are several gates to open and close, and herds of cows sometimes block the road.

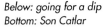

Star Attraction
•**Son Catlar**

Below: going for a dip
Bottom: Son Catlar

Map
on page
93

Cave paintings

An unusual place here is a prehistoric cave that has been adorned by its denizen, an artist named Nicolau Cabrisas – a sculptor and the *enfant terrible* of the holiday village. The cave contains imaginative ornaments, sculptures and masks (May to September, mornings).

SON SAURA

The idyllic bay of ★★ **Son Saura** has a very long, sandy beach, and its shallow waters are perfect for families with young children, with the adjacent pine forest providing welcome shade. From the eastern edge of the bay, the Cap des Talaier can be reached in a quarter of an hour. To reach the Cap d'Artrutx you either need to walk westwards along the beach or drive back to Ciutadella.

CALA SANTANDRIA AND OTHER BAYS

Several of the beaches on the southwest coast are strikingly beautiful, and attracted the attention of developers long ago. This explains the uninspired architecture in many places: holiday villages line up together side by side, with a few large hotels in between, and numerous bars and restaurants all competing for custom. As a result, the bays and beaches tend to get packed.

A first impression is provided by the beach at ★ **Cala Santandría**; if you can't find a space here the best thing to do is walk either north or south and try your luck at the next beach instead. The entrance to Cala Santandría is guarded by the 18th-century, British-built **Torre des Castell**.

From here it's only a stone's throw to the holiday settlement of **Cala Blanca**. Sunshades stand on the narrow beach in long lines, and high pine trees provide the apartments with shade. At the end of the bay are the remains of a prehistoric house, its ground-plan similar to that of a *naveta*. Ceramic finds have dated the place to between 2000 and 1000BC. There's a good view of the entire Menorcan west coast from the promontory of S'Aigo Dolca, located further to the south.

Santandría resort

CAP D'ARTRUTX

As the road continues southwards it is lined by walled-in fields, and two *talayots* can be seen to the left and right. Tall heaps of stones everywhere make it clear how hard it is to farm on Menorca – it's impossible to till even a metre of land without having to remove a large number of rocks and stones first. Roughly 3km (1½ miles) beyond Cala Blanca, a footpath leads off to the left and down to the bay of Son Saura.

If visibility is reasonably good, there is an incomparable view of the peaks on Mallorca from **Cap d'Artrutx**. The distance between the two Balearic Islands is 20 nautical miles, equivalent to 37km (23 miles). The black-and-white-striped lighthouse on the island's southwestern-most point was built in 1868, but is unfortunately closed to visitors.

Star Attraction
•**Son Saura**

Below: market trader
Bottom: Cap d'Artrutx

CALA EN BOSC

The next holiday village, **Cala en Bosc**, is especially popular with package tourists because of its 300-m (985-ft) beach and excellent recreational infrastructure. Whatever you want – surfboards, sailboats, motorboats, discos, karaoke bars, hostess bars – it's all here. A marina, a palm-lined promenade and large hotels and ethnic restaurants such as Bahia or Chinatown round off the general picture. If this place is too busy for you, take the *minitren* (a tourist train on tyres rather than rails) to the housing development at **Son Xoriguer** and discover the small beaches there, broken up by rocks. The architecture isn't that much different from the Cala en Bosc, however. Or you can set off back to Ciutadella.

Map
on page
93

8: The Rugged Northwest Coast

**Cala Morell – Platjes d'Algaiarens – Punta Nati
– Cala en Blanes – Los Delfines – Pont d'en Gil
– Ciutadella (50km/31 miles)**

The difference couldn't be more striking: to the
north of Ciutadella there are remote, barren and
almost depressing regions while close by to the
west the whitewashed holiday villages are located
side by side – although the areas where mass
tourism has made the most inroads tend to look
rather depressing, too.

*Below: shade against the sun
Bottom: Cala Morell bay*

Ciutadella, the former metropolis, serves as the
starting-point and end of this route. The side roads
leading to the sea sometimes pass less attractive
parts of Menorca, but the steep, rocky coast, up
to 40m (130ft) high in places, is always an experience in itself, whether it's the Cala Morell with
its weird rock formations, the Punta Nati, where
a lighthouse has warned mariners of underwater
dangers since 1913, or the Pont d'en Gil, a natural bridge eroded by centuries of seawater.

One special highlight of western Menorca are
the *barraques*, cattle shelters that look very similar to many of the island's prehistoric structures.

Broad and seemingly endless beaches like the
Platjes d'Algaiarens to the north are the exception here. The beaches west of the town are hardly
worthy of the name, and holidaymakers here tend
to favour their swimming pools.

LEAVING CIUTADELLA

From the centre of Ciutadella *(see page 35)*, the
way to Cala Morell and to the Platjes d'Algaiarens is not that easy to find. If you follow the
Contramurada – the ring road that follows the
course of the former town wall – the road to
Avinguda de La Constitució is signposted. A
bumpy asphalt road leads through the industrial area of Ciutadella and then past gardens and
fields edged with the drystone walls that are so
typical of the island. Here in the stony northwest
of the island the walls are frequently just a few
metres apart. With a little luck you may see a few

pedrers at work – the people who build and repair the walls with so much skill.

Torre d'en Quart

CALA MORELL

Beyond the Torre d'en Quart farm with theme-dieval watchtower that once served as a defence against pirate attack, the vegetation is replaced almost entirely by a stony desert, until the ★ **Cala Morell** and its tiny beach appear. The bay is surrounded by some very strange rock formations. They are part limestone and part conglomerate, and red blocks of sandstone can also be seen among them. This natural, weatherbeaten stone

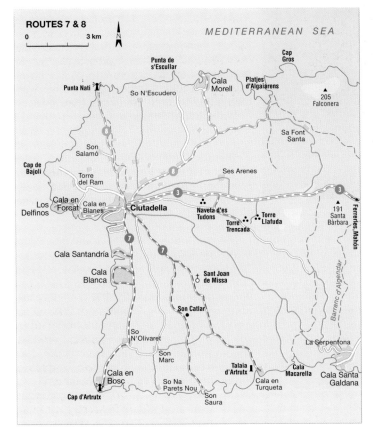

ROUTES 7 & 8

0   3 km

MEDITERRANEAN SEA

Punta de s'Escullar

Cap Gros

Punta Nati

So N'Escudero

Cala Morell

Platjes d'Algaiarens

205 Falconera

Sa Font Santa

Son Salamó

Cap de Bajoli

Torre del Ram

Ses Arenes

Los Delfinos

Cala en Forcat

Cala en Blanes

Ciutadella

Naveta d'es Tudons

Torre Trencada

Torre Llafuda

191 Santa Bàrbara

Ferreríes-Mahón

Cala Santandría

Cala Blanca

Sant Joan de Missa

Son Catlar

Barranc d'Algendar

So N'Olivaret

Son Marc

La Serpentona

Cala en Bosc

So Na Parets Nou

Talaia d'Artrutx

Cala en Turqueta

Cala Macarella

Cala Santa Galdana

Cap d'Artrutx

Son Saura

Map on page 93

garden dates back to the era when mighty mountains of mud rolled here from inland and then solidified. Wind and water then did the rest. Colour contrast is provided by the white houses in the developments of Son Morell and Marina. In the summer, boat trips are available from here along the steep coastline to the west, where you can go for lengthy clifftop walks. The levelled rock platforms below the cliffs are jokingly referred to as sunbeds

Above the bay, the original inhabitants of Menorca established a cave settlement dating back to around 3,000 years ago. The settlement consists of a total of 17 residential and funerary caverns, some of which are sub-divided into several smaller chambers. The Bronze and Iron Age caves are surprisingly refined, decorated with classical carvings and with windows cut into the rock; oval niches in the stone probably served as places to bury bones, and others to collect rainwater. The natural stone vaults of the caves look almost man-made as they spring from the floor on stout stone columns.

Below: Cala Morell caves
Bottom: Punta Nati

PLATJES D'ALGAIARENS

To the east of Cala Morell is the region of **La Vall**, the largest intact area of woodland on the island, renowned for its scenic beauty. The road leads

right through the middle as far as the fine, sandy ★ **Platjes d'Algaiarens**, where twin beaches are set in a horseshoe bay. The forests, bays and pine-lined beaches here are all privately owned, and the owner even has a security service patrolling the area to ensure that people stay out.

Up to 200 vehicles a day are allowed to pass through (toll payable) and use the car park near the beach – anyone in excess of that number is turned away. Pedestrians and cyclists are allowed through without any restrictions, however. From the car park, a short walk through the woods leads to the dunes from where you can clamber down onto the first beach. If this is too full, try the second or third beaches. There are no service amenities provided, nor is there any alternative way of getting back to Ciutadella – you must go back the way you came.

> **Barraques**
> One real attraction on the road to Punta Nati are the numerous *barraques* – cattle shelters resembling oversized snail-shells, built in a style reminiscent of the pre-historic *navetes* and *talayots*. Most date from the early 19th century, but some are more recent. Some *barraques* are even used as emergency accommodation by field labourers.

PUNTA NATI

If you follow the Contramurada ring road in Ciutadella as far as the caper-covered Bastió de sa Font and then turn off to the right, the road to Punta Nati cannot be missed.

This trip will introduce you to some of the less pleasant aspects of Menorca. A bumpy, potholed asphalt road leads past a scrap-heap and the largest refuse dump in the west of the island, and things can get pretty nasty if the wind happens to be blowing in the wrong direction. But if you can ignore the smell, and enjoy looking at landscapes that are practically devoid of vegetation, then this region is for you. The traditional Menorcan walls are everywhere, yet again, and sheep can be seen searching the barren ground for something to graze on.

From the northern cape of ★ **Punta Nati** the lighthouse of the same name has been sending its light across the waves ever since 1913. Be warned, if the gate happens to be closed, there's nowhere to turn round. But the 40-m (130-ft) high steep cliffs provide some excellent views across land and water, as well as the waves crashing against the reefs offshore.

Punta Nati lighthouse

Map
on page
93

*Below: cycling in the heat
Bottom: a greeting from
Los Delfines*

BAY OF THE DEAD

If you continue eastwards, past the cattle shelters which concealed artillery positions during the Spanish Civil War, the road leads past the Cala Es Pous and the **Cala Es Morts** – the Bay of the Dead' – which was where the French steamer *Général Chanzy* was wrecked on the rocks in 1910. Only one man survived the wreck in which 151 unfortunate passengers and crew members perished. The rusty old hulk of the vessel still commemorates the tragedy today.

TOURIST ENCLAVES

On the way back to Ciutadella there's another good site for fans of all things prehistoric: opposite the scrap-yard a track leads past a cattle-shed resembling a stepped pyramid. From there a narrow path leads to a field, to the remains of a megalithic village and above all to the *talayot* of **Torre Vella**, which has an entrance.

The way to the tourist enclaves of **Cala en Blanes**, **Cala en Forcat** and **Los Delfines** is signposted from the centre of Bastió de sa Font onwards. Outside Ciutadella, several cycle paths – rare on Menorca – can be seen at the side of the winding road. The rocky coast is covered with holiday houses, holiday settlements and holiday villages, where swimming pools, tennis courts, restaurants, discotheques and karaoke bars all blend into one vast tourism and entertainment complex. From the steep coast here there are several fine views, however: Mallorca can be seen in good weather, as can the lighthouse at Cap d'Artrutx, the southwestern-most point of the island.

BAY AND BEACHES

The bays with their miniature beaches lie at the centres of the various holiday enclaves, with the most generously-proportioned probably being the **Cala en Blanes**, which also has a small palm grove. The town of **Cala en Forcat** is grouped around the bay of the same name, with its numerous natural and concrete sun terraces. Not much of the beach can be seen when the trippers come here in peak season and lie packed together side by side like sardines. Small fountains spurt out of the rock now and then – they're not volcanic, but the result of pressure changes in a subterranean system of caverns.

PONT D'EN GIL

If you walk from the Hipodromo racecourse on the outskirts of **Los Delfines** in a northwesterly direction along the coast for about 10 minutes, you will reach the ★ **Pont d'en Gil** promontory with its large rocky gateway, which was carved out by the sea. It immediately makes you want to stop and picnic nearby or slip through the archway on a small boat.

If you still don't feel too weary from all the walking, why not carry on to the **Cap de Bajolí** further north? A defensive tower dating from the 17th century, built here as part of an early warning system against pirate incursions, will guide you on your way.

On the way back to Ciutadella, take a look at the posters outside the Hipodromo. Horse races are usually held here at weekends, and are always well patronised. Bets are taken too, of course. *¡Que tenga suerte!* (Good luck!)

Aqua Park
If you've got young children, you can take them to the Aqua Park in Cala Forcat, where they are sure to enjoy the flumes and slides. The restaurant serves excellent pizzas and there's also a bouncy castle play area. The entrance fee is for the whole day but you can come and go as you please. Open 10am–6pm, the park can be found on the main road going into Cala Forcat from Ciutadella; there is also a bus which drops you right outside the entrance.

Pont d'en Gil

Architectural heritage

If the official count is correct, there are more than 1,600 prehistoric monuments on Menorca. They include natural caverns that were inhabited over 5,000 years ago, caves cut out of limestone with great difficulty, watchtowers, funerary buildings and entire villages. There are 2½ archaeological sites per square kilometre, so Menorca can rightly be termed an open-air museum – Mallorca, Ibiza and Formentera all fall far behind. And since archaeology is a relatively young science, it can be assumed that a great deal remains to be discovered on the island. By the end of the 1940s around 500 sites were known about, but that figure had risen to 1,000 a decade later.

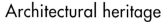

Cave dwellings
The evidence from the megalithic period raises more questions than it answers. It seems certain, however, that the first settlers sailed from the coast of Southern France and arrived on the northernmost of the Balearic Islands in around 5000BC. Natural caves in bays such as Cales Coves, Cala Morell and Cala Canutells, or the gigantic Cova d'es Coloms in the interior, all provided these early visitors with welcome accommodation. The more people they had to house, the more antechambers, niches and additional rooms were created. Many of the caves were built completely by human beings, and were used as living accommodation, burial grounds, or a mixture of the two.

MEGALITHIC STRUCTURES

Menorca developed its main reputation as an archaeological treasure-trove from the megalithic structures known as *talayots, taules* and *navetas*, which were built quite independently from any cave settlements between 2000 and 800BC. During this period a civilisation developed in the Western Mediterranean that has become known on the Balearic Islands as the *Talayotic* culture.

Opposite: Taula de Trepucó
Below: Talayot de Torrellonet

TALAYOTS

This period was named after the *talayots* – stone towers, usually round, and up to 10m (32ft) high. The name possibly comes from *atalaya*, the Arabic word for a watchtower. Comparable to the *torri* of Corsica or the *nuraghi* of Sardinia, they were probably used not only as watchtowers but also as refuges in time of danger; they could also have provided accommodation for village elders, and subsequently served as burial sites for them.

Around 200 *talayots* have survived on Menorca. There are interesting ones in the settlements of Talati de Dalt, Torre d'en Galmes Son Catlar and Trepucó. The highest tower is the one at Torrellonet, which has been equipped with flight guidance systems for the nearby airport.

The most impressive interior, complete with stone pillars and beams, can be seen at the site of Sant Agustí Vell *(see page 82)*.

TAULES

Taules (the Menorcan word for tables) are T-shaped stone structures composed of two massive stone slabs, one above the other. Over 30 of them still exist on Menorca, and lie at the centre of any megalithic settlement. Their original purpose is not known, but the *taules*, which are up to 5m (16ft) high, are always located at the very centre of horseshoe-shaped patterns of monolithic stones in temple areas, where traces of fires and benches for animal sacrifices have also been discovered. The most impressive *taules* can be seen at Torralba d'en Salort, Talatí de Dalt, Torre Trencada, Trepucó, Son Catlar and Torre Llisà Vell.

NAVETES

The third kind of prehistoric structure on Menorca is the *naveta,* an ossuary reminiscent of a boat lying keel-upwards, hence the name. These structures contain an antechamber, a large interment chamber on ground level and frequently a burial chamber above it. The only way to enter a *naveta* is on one's hands and knees. The amount of bones found inside them makes it likely that they were used as tribal tombs, and many contained valuable funerary offerings such as rings, amulets, necklaces and small figurines. The Navetes de Rafal Rubí and the Naveta d'es Tudons are the most remarkable monuments of their type, and the latter is also believed to be the oldest structure in the whole of Spain.

LATER DEVELOPMENTS

There are few remnants of classical antiquity on Menorca, but both the Greeks and the Phoenicians left behind evidence of trading activity in the form of jewellery, utensils and coins. The Phoenicians and the Romans had great respect for the

Below: Talatí de Dalt
Bottom: Naveta d'es Tudons

Balearides (the name given to the islanders because of their throwing ability – *ballein* is the Greek word for throw). The sling was a vital weapon the islanders employed against foreign foes, and the slingsmen of Menorca were recruited as mercenaries, constituting an important division in Hannibal's armies as well as in the Roman force that conquered Carthage in 143BC.

ROMANS, CHRISTIANS AND MOORS

Under Quintus Caecilius Metellus, the Romans finally conquered the islands in 123BC. They fortified the local strongholds, constructed villas, baths and temples, and of course built their roads, such as the one that can still be seen on Puig de Santa Agueda *(see page 59)*. After the collapse of the Roman Empire, the Balearics were subjected to continuous plundering, and it was only after 1025 that a new cultural heyday emerged under the Moors. However, not many Arab buildings survived the Christian conquest at the beginning of the 13th century; most of them were either destroyed or incorporated into new structures. Ciutadella's main mosque, for example, became the Gothic cathedral. The Gothic pointed arch replaced the horseshoe arch of the Moors, but the Spanish did adopt the Moorish idea of arcaded courtyards and fountains, where water allowed.

Mystery of the *taules*
How the incredibly heavy stones of the *taules* were placed on top of each other and connected without any technological assistance remains a mystery to this day, as does their significance. Did they represent deities, or were they used to mark cult sites?

Església del Roser in Ciutadella

In the Middle Ages, most building activity was of a religious nature, but later on magnificent secular buildings were constructed by merchants, landowners and wealthy artisans. Townhouses and *palazzi* were built in Ciutadella. With their richly decorated façades and beautiful courtyards, these buildings represented a fusion of the many different styles that came together in the Balearics, and some of them can still be admired today.

MENORCA'S FARMHOUSES

Crossing Menorca, you can't fail to notice all the white-washed farmhouses. Some might dominate a hilltop while others occupy a more modest position, stooped low against the ground as if cowering against the elements – braced for an onslaught of the north wind, the *tramuntana*. But whatever their location, these farmhouses all share a distinctive Menorcan style of architecture.

The central yards of these *llocs* are invariably surrounded by several buildings, which is why the locals refer to them in the plural, as *ses cases* – the houses. The northern side is usually occupied by outbuildings such as stables and dairies, which help protect the rest of the farm from the elements. Living quarters always face south, as does the patio area, which is usually furnished with a well, an oven for baking, a water trough and a round threshing floor made of brick. The entire complex is surrounded by a dry-stone wall.

Also typical is the protruding triple-arched porch area *(sa porxada)*; in the summer this is the focus of family life and in winter the venue for traditional livestock slaughtering and festivities *(matanzas)*. The roof of this porch doubles as a terrace. The shallow gable roof is in the typical Spanish style with terracotta tiles; terracotta pipes carry the water to underground storage cisterns.

The *llocs* are built of large limestone slabs *(marés)* obtained from the island's quarries. As the limestone is porous and lacks water resistance, the walls are treated with a coat of whitewash once a year, adding flashes of brightness to Menorca's already broad spectrum of colours.

Below: Ciutadella townhouses

Festivals

Steeped in centuries of tradition, Menorca's festivals are spectacular events, including fireworks, horse dancing and processions.

January 17: Fests d'es Tres Tocs, or festival of the three blows, held in Ciutadella to commemorate the *Reconquista* of Menorca in 1287.

March/April: Semana Santa, or Easter Week, at its most impressive in Maó and Ciutadella: religious celebrations and processions.

June 23 and 24: Festes de Sant Joan, the festival of St John, held in Ciutadella. Two days of equestrian fun, including the *jaleo (*horses' dance) on the Plaça d'es Born, which is crowned by a magnificent fireworks display. This is Menorca's most lively festival *(see also page 37).*

July: On the **15th and 16th** boat processions in Maó, Ciutadella and Fornells. In the island's harbours the **Virgen del Carmen**, the patron saint of mariners and fishermen, is celebrated in colourful processions. On the third weekend in July is the **Festa de Sant Martí,** or festival of St Martin, with horseback processions and tournaments plus the traditional *jaleo*. On the fourth weekend is the **Festa de Sant Antoní** in Antonells in honour of the patron saint. The processions are crowned by a magnificent *jaleo* at the harbour.

August: A whole series of local **patron saint celebrations**, featuring processions and, especially, markets. The first weekend has celebrations in Es Migjorn Gran, the second in Alaior, the third in Sant Climent and the fourth in Sant Lluís, while Ferreries celebrates its saint on August 24 and 25.

September: 7th to 9th, Festes de la Vierge de Gracia, the festival of the Holy Virgin of Monte Toro, held in Maó; processions and a horseback parade with around 100 horses, all crowned by the biggest fireworks display on the island.

Below: jaleo in Ciutadella
Bottom: Festes de Gracia figure
Overleaf: local restaurant sign

RESTAURANTE

EL GALLO

FOOD AND DRINK

Menorca has a vast amount of delicious culinary delights. The overladen market stalls in the Claustre del Carme in Maó or at the Mercat in Ciutadella all prompt you to visit the nearest gourmet restaurant, especially in Es Mercadal or Es Migjorn Gran. Many meals begin with fresh bread and a small bowl of *alioli*, mayonnaise in its original form *(see overleaf)*. This overture is followed by the revelations of a hearty, filling and calorie-rich cuisine – as long as you stay away from any establishments boasting 'international cooking', which usually means there will be pizza, chips and hamburgers on the menu.

SEAFOOD ASSORTMENT

Top of the popularity list are the seafood dishes, especially *caldereta de langosta*, which is especially good in the restaurants of Fornells. A thick soup is prepared over high heat using tomatoes, onions, garlic, parsley, leek, a little cognac, and thinly sliced lobster, then poured onto slices of bread and served. Each cook refines the dish differently according to a personal recipe that is naturally kept secret. The only disadvantage of this superb dish is its price – you won't get one for less than around €28.

The *caldereta* family also includes two cheaper dishes, however: *caldereta de mariscos*, a shellfish soup, and *caldereta de pescado*, which contains several different kinds of fish. Lovers of fish will also be pleased to find pike, swordfish and perch on the menus here. A typically Menorcan variant is to bake the fish in the oven with potatoes and halved tomatoes.

Anyone who is eager to try a number of different kinds of fish should sample a *parillada de pescado*, which is varied and delicious. The island's cooks are just as good at shellfish and crustaceans: squid, mussels and seasnails are all expertly prepared.

Paella, the most popular tourist dish, can contain both fish *(paella marinera)* and meat. However, the classic ones usually feature saffron rice, chicken, pork, mussels, shrimps, cuttlefish, beans and peas.

FURTHER SPECIALITIES

Like their colleagues on the mainland, Menorcan cooks use a lot of onions, garlic and olive oil, but these are

Mahón Cheese

If the souvenir shops had anything to do with it, every visitor to Menorca would take home at least one *Queso de Mahón*. Regardless of the aroma and oppressive summer heat, no souvenir shop would be complete without a row of these colourfully packed cheeses.

Some of Menorca's cheese is still made by small family businesses, but most is now produced on a large scale. Since 1985, it has all carried the official label *Queso de Mahón*, although Alaior is actually the centre of production. Despite mechanisation, the cheese is still made in the traditional manner, except that cow's milk rather than sheep's milk is used. First, the whey is separated from the set milk using muslin. The cheese is then soaked for a day in salt water and left on a rack for a month where it is turned. A mix of butter, olive oil and paprika is then applied to the surface, and 2 months later the cheese is ready. According to maturity, the taste varies from tangy to spicy and the colour from deep yellow to ivory. After 8 months it has a similar texture to parmesan.

Queso de Mahón is best bought either straight from the farm or from a factory outlet in Alaior. You won't get the colourful packaging but you may get a glimpse of the cellars, and the price is lower than in souvenir shops.

enhanced by local ingredients such as cream, butter and *Queso de Mahón* *(see previous page)*. Ingredients common to many meat dishes include capers, figs, cabbage, beans and artichokes. The meat ranges from pork and beef to rabbit, quail and partridge.

Whether i 's *conejo con higos* (rabbit with dried figs) or *cordero con cebollas y alcaparras* (lamb with onions and capers), these oven-baked dishes are among the true highlights of Menorcan cuisine – especially if you happen to order them from the Ca n'Aguedet restaurant in Es Mercadal or El Gallo near Ferreries.

Special island delicacies include stuffed aubergines, peppers, courgettes and artichokes as well as the numerous simple soups enjoyed by the rural population, available in every pub: *oliaigua*, a vegetable soup consisting of tomatoes, onions, cabbage and toasted bread comes in all kinds of variations. The vegetable stew known as *tumbet*, baked with a cheese topping, contains sections of fried aubergine and potato.

Tapas, the famous Spanish appetisers, can be found in all variations on Menorca. Portions of fried squid , *albóndigas* (meat balls), spicy *chorizo*, and *butifarrone*, white or black sausages, are among the most famous. Tapas are often accompanied by *pa amb tomàquet*, bread rubbed with oil, garlic and tomato. Good snacks, which are also eaten as desserts, include *amargos* (almond-flavoured biscuits) and *ensaimadas* (yeast cakes fried in lard and topped with icing sugar), which are popular for breakfast.

THE SECRET OF MAYONNAISE

Menorcan still-lifes very often contain certain ingredients: eggs, half a lemon, a small bottle of olive oil, several cloves of garlic and a little salt. There is a special reason for this: the thick sauce known as *alioli*, served tepid, consists of these ingredients and was invented on Menorca. In 1756 the French had just driven the British (temporarily) from the island, and their leader, the Duke of Richelieu, wanted to celebrate the occasion.

A local cook created the exquisite sauce, the French adored it, took the recipe to Paris and left out the garlic, which may have contributed greatly to the global triumph of *salsa mahonesa*, better known as mayonnaise.

In another version of the story, the cook was a mistress of Richelieu's. In memory of his amorous escapade, he is reputed to have named this culinary speciality after the place where he met the *mahonesa* he had loved.

DRINKS

If you need something to settle your stomach after all this indulgence, try the *hierbas* – herbal liqueur that tastes of camomile – or *calent*, an aniseed, cinnamon and saffron liqueur that is drunk warm. The *palo* – a bitter-tasting brew made of gentian extract and various oriental herbs – is regarded as a stimulant. For something really refreshing, there is the local-brand *Xoriguer* gin, served in a 1:3 mixture with lemonade that is called a *pomada*.

Restaurant selection

The following restaurants on Menorca have been subdivided into three categories: €€€ = expensive, €€ = moderately priced, € = inexpensive.

Alaior

The Cobblers, Carrer de San Macario 6, tel: 971 37 14 00. An English-run restaurant in a converted cobbler's shop, with good chicken dishes and excellent salads. €€

Ximenes, Carrer Dr Albinana 2, tel: 971 37 11 20. This is a simple, smoky basement pub which serves delicious food that is both filling and cheap. **€**

Arenal d'en Castell
La Paella, Plaza de Mar 1, tel: 971 35 80 65. Right above the beach, with a terrace; lots of fish and meat dishes, liberally spiced with garlic. **€€€**

Biniancolla
Biniancolla, tel: 908 099061. Large restaurant terrace above the bay, great for dining at sunset, lots of seafood specialities, and great *paella*. **€€**

Binibeca Vell
El Pescadito, tel: 971 18 85 43. Pleasant place with vaulted ceiling, and large selection of fresh fish. **€€**
Bini Grill, tel: 971 15 05 94. Rustic restaurant with enormous Serrano hams hanging from the ceiling, and a shady inner courtyard. **€€**

Cala Marina
Cala Marina, Cala Molí 2, tel: 908-63 82 99. Beautiful restaurant above the bay with a roof terrace, numerous fish dishes, and massive *paellas*. **€€**

Cala Santa Galdana
La Cala, tel: 971 37 32 47. Has a viewing terrace, great seafood, and free *tapas* if you order a drink. **€€**
Es Barranc, Cala Santa Galdana, tel: 971 15 46 43. Right at the entrance to the Barranc d'Algendar, and the food is good despite the uninspired furnishings; try the fish balls. **€€**
El Mirador, tel: 908-79 98 47, uninspiring mass fare, but the location on a promontory off the bay is utterly superb. **€**

Cala Santandría
Sa Nacra, Cala Sa Caleta, tel: 971 38 62 06. Cave restaurant with Spanish cuisine on the next bay to the north of Cala Santandría. **€€**

Ciutadella
El Bribón, Marina 115, tel: 971 38 50 50. One of the most famous restaurants in the harbour, mainly does fish dishes. **€€**
Casa Manolo, Marina 117, tel: 971 38 00 03. Another popular seafood restaurant in the harbour, with air-conditioning, terrace and magnificent views. **€€**
Ca's Quintu, Plaça de Alfons III 4, tel: 971 38 10 02. A sunny restaurant with view of an old mill; the *boquerones en vinagre* (fresh anchovies in vinegar) are particularly good. **€**
Café Balear, Port de Ciutadella, tel: 971 38 00 05. Offers a good, reasonably priced set menu. **€€**

Es Mercadal
Ca n'Aguedet, Carrer Lepanto 23 and 30, tel: 971 37 53 91. Excellent rabbit, lamb and suckling pig dishes. The owners, the Vadell family, also produce the only wine on the island. **€€**
Ca n'Olga, Pont de na Macarrana, tel: 971 37 54 59. Hidden away behind an arch near the Torrente, with large garden terrace and stylish furnishings; very good Menorcan food, especially the seafood, quail and rabbit. **€€**
Molis d'es Reco, Carrer Vicario Fuxà

> **Water and wine**
> The water on Menorca is perfectly safe to drink but it has a rather distinctive taste. Most people drink bottled water – *agua mineral*. If you want it sparkling, ask for *agua con gas*, while still water is *agua sin gas*. *Fresca* means chilled, *natural* means straight off the shelf. Wine is usually drunk with meals, but as there is only one local producer – the Vadell family who own the Can'Aguedet (*see above*), it nearly all comes from mainland Spain. Beer, both bottled and draught, is more popular with younger people.

53, tel: 971 37 53 92, old mill restaurant with a large terrace on the C721 that specialises in catering to large coach parties. €

Es Migjorn Gran

Migjorn, Carrer Major, tel: 971 37 01 12. House with small courtyard terrace and select Menorcan dishes, all refined in an interesting way. €

S'Engolidor, Carrer Major 3, tel: 971 37 01 93. Great Menorcan dishes and a view over the gorge. Reservations essential. €€

Ferreries

El Gallo, Cta. Cala Santa Galdana, tel: 971 37 30 39. Old farmhouse restaurant serving good grilled meat. €€

Liorna, Carrer de Dalt 9, tel: 971 37 38 89. A nice little pizzeria, which also hosts interesting art exhibitions. €€

Fornells

Es Cranc, Carrer Escorles 31, tel: 971 37 64 42. Large, light establishment with excellent fish and a cheap lunchtime set menu. €€

El Pescador, Plaça s'Algaret 3, tel: 971 37 65 38. There are ceramic plates with crustacean motifs on the walls, and a huge fish menu, as well as a pleasant terrace and promenade. €€

Es Pla, Pasaje des Plá, tel: 971 37 66 55. Tastefully decorated seafood restaurant right beside the lagoon. Apparently King Juan Carlos sampled a *caldereta* here once. €€

Maó

Club Maritimo, Moll de Llevant 27, tel: 971 36 42 26. Elegant harbour-side restaurant serving delicious seafood, cooked to local, often experimental, recipes. Has a large terrace. €€€

Alba, Moll de Llevant 298, tel: 971 35 06 06. Good island cooking and attractive views. €€

Ca Na Pilar, Carrer Cardona y Orfila 61, tel: 971 36 68 17. Traditionl dishes of high quality; fish plus lamb and chicken. €€

Casa del Mar, Moll de Ponent 112, tel: 971 35 07 42. Delicious fish, large helpings, too. €

Il Porto, Moll de Llevant 225, tel: 971 35 44 26. Busy place, with a huge menu. €

La Tropical, Luna 36, tel: 971 36 05 56. Island dishes at a price that won't hurt your budget. €

Roma, Moll de Llevant 295, tel: 971 35 37 77. Most popular pizzeria in Maó, and the pizzas are absolutely enormous. €

San Tomás

Es Bruc, Carretera San Adeoato, tel: 971 37 04 88. Meals served on a large terrace above the beach; good selection of *tapas*. €

Sant Climent

Casino Sant Climent, Carrer de Sant Jaume 4, tel: 971 15 34 18. Simple food, served to the accompaniment of good jazz on Tuesday and Thursday, when musicians are welcome to bring their own instruments and join in. €

Sant Lluís

Pan y Vino, Torret 52, tel: 971 15 03 22. This is *the* place for Menorcan cuisine and select wines. Set in the village of Torret, near Sant Lluís, it is elegant, intimate, and very popular with the local expatriate population. €€€

El Picadero, Cta Maó–San Lluis, tel: 971 36 32 68. British-run restaurant with a barbecue and lots of meat. €€

La Venta, Carrer de Sant Lluís, tel: 971 15 09 95. Rustically furnished restaurant/bar with traditional Menorcan cuisine. €€

La Rueda, Carrer de Sant Lluís 30, tel: 971 15 11 84. A friendly bar with dishes typical of the island and a varied selection of *tapas*. €

ACTIVE HOLIDAYS

BEACHES

Despite some wonderful hiking routes and the 9-hole golf course of Son Bou, the sea is naturally the focal point of tourist interest on Menorca.

The island has bays and beaches to suit every taste, and they really are picturesque. There are huge differences, however: on the Platja de Son Bou or the Cala Santa Galdana with their high-rise hotels, be prepared to share the beach with many others. Things are far quieter on the beaches known as *platjes verges* to the southeast of Ciutadella. Not all the beaches can be easily reached by car, and the last section often has to be done on foot. Bays like Cala en Turqueta, Cala des Talaier or Son Saura are worth walking to, in any case. Topless sunbathing is a common sight now (but do cover up when you leave the beach); nudism is still only possible in the most remote bays such as Cala Macarellata.

HIKING

Menorca is ideal for short or long hikes, and it's easy to orient yourself according to landmarks like Monte Toro or the Puig de Santa Àgueda. The best starting points for hikes are Ferreries, Alaior, Fornells and Es Mercadal. A word of warning, however: many of the routes are not properly marked, and even expensive maps leave a lot to be desired. The best maps are those from the Servicio Geográfico del Ejército, on scales of 1:50 000 and 1:25 000 respectively. You can get them in bookshops in Maó and Ciutadella if you show your passport.

The Camí de Cavalls *(see page 11)*, is also marked on these maps: in the north and southwest it leads through remote regions of great natural beauty. If you are crossing private property, be sure to close all gates and fences behind you so that farmers don't get annoyed.

For information on guided walks, contact the Oficina d'Informació Turística in Maó and Ciutadella *(see page 113)*. Bird-watching trips and other nature tours are organised by the GOB (Carrer d'Isabel II, 42, Maó, tel: 971 35 07 63).

CYCLING

Bikes can be hired from several shops in Ciutadella, Maó and most of the holiday centres. They cost around €4

Surfing and swiming at Cala en Porter

a day to hire. Mountain bikes are a better bet than touring bikes because quite a few roads and beach-access tracks are incredibly bumpy. You don't need to be particularly athletic or good at climbing gradients, however.

The old Camí d'en Kane *(see page 50)* and the Camí de Binifabini near Alaior in the north are easy and quiet.

RIDING

On Menorca, horses are either bred for racing or used as work animals; riding is purely for visitors. The meetings at racecourses in Maó and Ciutadella are well attended every week, because Menorcans are happier to bet on horses than to ride them. Day-long riding trips are available from around 20 stables, including the Rancho Allenwood (tel: 971 15 30 71) near Sant Climent and Club Hipic es Boeret (tel: 971 15 10 49) at S'Algar. The Hort de Llucaitx Park (Carretera Maó–Fornells, km 17, tel: 629 39 28 94), also has horses and ponies for hire.

WATERSPORTS

Menorca is ideal for windsurfers and sailors, whether beginners, keen amateurs or professionals. The holiday centres and marinas in the south of the island are the best places to head for. Punta Prima and the nearby Cala en Bosc are both very good for windsurfing. Fornells has a yacht club that offers surfing courses and rents out equipment, and it is perfectly located on a long bay. The club also has a sailing school and 50 berths.

The larger towns are also popular with watersports enthusiasts: the Club Náutico de Ciutadella (tel: 971 38 11 46), for instance, runs sailing courses lasting several weeks. The Club Marítimo de Maó (tel: 971 36 50 22) is also a good sailing school. The most ambitious of all of them is the Club S'Algar Diving and Watersports (tel: 971 15

06 01) in Cala d'Alcaufar, where you can learn anything from windsurfing to water-skiing with a paraglider. Lengthy diving sessions along the reefs and in the grottos of the rocky south coast; many are only accessible from underwater. The Diving Centre, Cala Torret, tel: 971 18 85 28 offers introductions to scuba as well as daily diving trips. Scuba Menorca (tel: 971 35 13 63) in Maó, is a recommended diving school. So is Diving Center Fornells, Passeig Marítim 44B, Fornells, tel: 971 376 431 in the north.

Nightlife
Nightlife roughly falls into two categories: the loud late-night action in the bigger resorts, where you will rub shoulders almost exclusively with other tourists; and the more indigenous spots, mostly in Maó and Ciutadella. The island's discos come and go in the popularity stakes (and are only open in summer). The old warehouse area behind the marina in Ciutadella throbs with noisy venues. Things don't get moving until late: some places don't open until 11pm but once open, they keep going.

A few bars and clubs that have stood the test of time are:

Akelaare, Moll de Ponent 42, Maó, tel: 971 36 85 20. Music and cocktails in an upmarket bar on the harbour.

Asere, Carrer Corniola 23, Ciutadella, tel 971 38 38 52. A salsa club where nothing happens until very late.

Casino Sant Climent, Carrer de Sant Jaume 4, tel: 971 15 34 18. Good jazz sessions on Tuesday and Thursday; musicians are welcome to bring their own instruments and join in.

El Salón, Carrer Victor 28, Es Castell. Satire, song, dance and excellent theatre by a small troupe, including female impersonaters.

Piano Bar, Carrer Sant Ignasi, Es Castell, tel: 971 36 40 22. As laid-back as it sounds.

PRACTICAL INFORMATION

Getting There

BY AIR

The quickest, most comfortable and also the cheapest way of reaching Menorca is by plane, with plenty of direct flights, both scheduled and chartered, from the main British airports. Flights to major Spanish destinations such as Barcelona, Palma de Mallorca or Madrid can sometimes be extended with an internal flight to Menorca using the Spanish airline Aviaco to Maó (to the airport located 7km/4 miles to the southwest of town), but the prices for scheduled flights are a lot higher, and there's quite a bit of waiting around involved, too. Make sure you confirm your departure flight in good time: in peak season, seats on planes can get snapped up quickly.

Travelling independently, choosing your own airline and hotel, usually works out more expensive than booking on a package tour because you lose the benefit of discounts that tour operators can negotiate. A ready-assembled holiday does not mean you have to be part of a regimented group; the only time you need be with your fellow travellers is during the flight and on the bus transferring you to and from your hotel.

BY SEA

Travelling by train or bus to Barcelona and then on to Menorca is so exhausting and expensive that few people are tempted to try it (20 hours journey, not including the boat). But if you're driving to Spain and feel like extending your holiday with a quick trip to Menorca, make sure you have your driving licence, insurance green card, the bail bond that comes with it, and vehicle documentation. Taking your own car to Menorca only starts to pay

off after around five days, however, because of the relatively high ferry price and the fact that hire cars on the island are quite cheap (roughly €25 a day, if booked in advance).

There are ferries several times a week in summer from Barcelona to Maó, and the crossing takes around nine hours. You can also reach Maó from Palma or Valencia. In peak season, or Easter week, it's best to reserve in good time (advance bookings from the principal ferry operator Trasmediterránea, Moll Comercial, Maó, tel: 971 36 60 50; tel: 902 45 46 45 in Barcelona; www.trasmediterranea.es, or from travel agents).

Passenger ferries from Mallorca run between Cala Ratjada and Ciutadella (Cape Balear Cruceros, tel: 971 81 85 17 www.cape-balear.com). The journey takes about 75 minutes and there are some good deals, including some that offer inclusive bus journeys to and from Palma. Car ferries run twice a day (except Saturday) between Port d'Alcúdia and Ciutadella and take around 2 hours 45 minutes (Iscomar Ferries; tel: 902 119 128; fax: 971 70 77 21 www.iscomar.com).

Getting Around

BY BUS

There is no railway on the island but the bus system is comprehensively structured. Red and white buses connect Maó and Ciutadella several times a day, and the intermediate stops are Alaior, Es Mercadal and Ferreries. Change in any of those towns and you can travel to the southern resorts.

Direct connections from Maó (grey and ancient buses) and Ciutadella (yellow buses) take care of connections to the north and south of each city. Prices are relatively cheap, and tickets are sold on the buses. The bus companies haven't quite synchronised their timetables, so if you're planning to make a connection, you may have a long wait. Hardly any buses operate on Sundays, either. Most of the prehistoric sites on Menorca can only be reached by car.

BY HIRE CAR, MOPED OR VESPA

Having a car on Menorca enables you to reach a lot of attractions that would otherwise be inaccessible. The island has few roads, however, and they get crowded, so you should drive with particular care in busy holiday periods. Spanish fuel prices are somewhat cheaper than in Britain. A hire car costs from around €25 a day for the smallest model, while a moped or a Vespa will set you back around €12.

All the major international rental companies (Atesa, Avis, Hertz and Europcar) have offices at the airports, as well as in Maó, Ciutadella and the various holiday resorts, as do reputable Spanish agencies. In Alaior, Es Castell and Es Mercadal the main providers are local firms. In the summer months it is advisable to pre-book your car hire before leaving home – this can be done cheaply via the Internet. Mopeds and Vespas, on the other hand, are usually available without advance reservation.

Rules of the Road

To hire a car or a moped a national driving licence is enough. Driving is on the right and seatbelts are obligatory both in the front and back of cars. Note that the C721, the road between Ciutadella and Maó, is the only one on the island where you can travel at 100kmph (62mph) because it's the widest; all other routes are considered country roads, and the maximum speed limit is 80kmph (50mph). Traffic police frequently stop drivers.

BY TAXI

The taxi drivers on Menorca have lists of fares for every route. Cabs can be found parked in marked ranks in most of the towns and resorts. If there doesn't happen to be one, just call the central number, tel: 971 36 71 11. Hotel receptionists are usually happy to call a taxi for you.

Facts for the Visitor

ENTRY REQUIREMENTS

British citizens and citizens of the US, Australia and New Zealand need a passport to enter Spain, while visitors from other EU countries require only a valid national identity card. For stays of more than 90 days, residence permits are required. Applications can be made at the Aliens Office in the appropriate province.

CUSTOMS

Duty-free allowances on imports from EU countries no longer exist, but do still apply to goods bought outside the EU. There are no restrictions on importing duty-paid goods bought in the EU provided they are for personal consumption. Duty-free allowances for non-EU travellers to Spain are 200 cigarettes (or 50 cigars), one litre of alcohol, 2 litres of wine, 250ml eau-de-cologne and 50g perfume.

There are no limits on the amount of money, Spanish or foreign, that you may import, although you should declare sums over the equivalent of €30,000.

TOURIST INFORMATION

The Spanish National Tourist Office will supply holiday information.
Spanish National Tourist Office, 22–23 Manchester Square, London W1U 3PX, tel: 020 7486 8077, fax: 020 7486 8034; brochure line, tel: 09063 640 630.

E-mail: info.londres@tourspain.es
Website: www.tourspain.co.uk
New York: 666 Fifth Avenue, New
York, NY 10103.Tel: 212-265 8822,
fax: 212-265 8864.
E-mail: nuevayork@tourspain.es
Website: www. okspain.org
On Menorca: Oficina d'Informació
Turística, Carrer Sa Rovellada de Dalt
24, Maó, tel: 971 36 37 90, fax: 971 36
60 56; Airport , tel: 971 15 71 15; Ofic-
ina d'Informació Turística, Plaça de la
Catedral, Ciutadella, tel: 971 38 26 93.

CURRENCY AND EXCHANGE
Spain's monetary unit is the euro (ab-
breviated €), which is divided into 100
cents. Bank notes are available in de-
nominations of 500, 200, 100, 50, 20,
10 and 5 euros. There are coins for 1
and 2 euros and for 50, 20, 10, 5, 2 and
1 cent.

The easiest way to obtain cash is
with a credit or debit card and a PIN
number at one of the many ATM
machines *(telebancos)* on the island.
Many shops and most restaurants and
hotels accept credit cards, mainly
MasterCard, Eurocard and Visa, but it
is wise to check in advance. Practically
all Spanish banks will change foreign
currency and travellers' cheques. They
offer the best rates and little or no com-
mission, but rates can vary from bank
to bank so it is worth shopping around.
Always take your passport when you
go to change money.

TIPPING
Many restaurants now automatically
add a 10 percent tip *(propina)* to the
bill. In a bar or café it is usual to leave
a few coins for the waiter. Hotel
chamber-maids usually expect a sum
appropriate to your length of stay,
porters around 50 cents per item of
luggage carried. When travelling by
taxi, add 10 percent or else try to
round up the fare.

OPENING TIMES
Shops are usually open from 9.30am
to 1.30pm and 5– 8pm, Saturday until
1pm. Food shops open a little earlier,
supermarkets often stay open all day
until 10pm.

Banks are open Monday to Friday
9am–1 or 2pm, but *bureaux de change*
have longer opening hours, and sometimes open on Saturday morning.

Post offices are open Monday to Saturday 9am–1pm, 4–6pm, and in Maó
and Ciutadella on weekdays till 9pm.

PUBLIC HOLIDAYS
January 1 (New Year's Day), Janu-
ary 6 (Epiphany), January 17 (Sant
Antoni – Commemoration of the
Reconquista in 1287), May 1 (Labour
Day), July 25 (Sant Jaume, Spain's

Arts and crafts
The sheer variety of Menorcan arts
and crafts can be appreciated at the
fairs and markets in Ciutadella and Maó: tables
covered with hand-made shoes, sandals and
belts; fashion jewellery; studded handbags; plus
jugs, plates and amphorae, and the prices are
usually very reasonable.

The leather sandals called *abarcas* are very
popular: always the same shape, they come in
different colours and can be made for men and
women individually. The sole is made of leather;
a broad leather strap covers the foot, leaving
the toes free; and a smaller, narrower strap
encircles the ankle.

Menorcan potters make a great variety of
products. Their trademarks are the *bótils* and
ollas – clay bottles and pots in different shapes
and sizes, with unglazed exteriors. Several
more colourful types have historically based
patterns and ornamentation on the outside;
many of the plates and pots have island landscapes on them.If you want to watch potters and
painters at work, go to the harbour section of
Maó and look for the Alfarería Menorquina.

patron saint), August 15 (Assumption), October 12 (Virgen del Pilar, patron saint of the Guardia Civil, and also Columbus Day), November 1 (All Saints'), December 8 (Immaculate Conception), December 25 and 26 (Christmas). There are also several moveable feasts such as Maundy Thursday, Good Friday, Easter Monday, Whit Monday and Corpus Christi.

Sant Joan

The feast of Sant Joan, described on page 37, isn't an official public holiday, but don't expect anything to be functioning normally in Ciutadella, where ordinary life in the town grinds to a halt.

Post

Stamps *(sellos)* are available from the post offices *(correos)* in Maó, Ciutadella, Alaior and Es Castell, from tobacconists *(estancos/tabacs)* all over the island, and from many places that sell postcards.

TELEPHONING

The code for Spain is 00 34.To dial the UK from Spain, prefix your number with 00 44 and omit the first zero from the area code.

The easiest way to make a phone call is at a Telefónica office where you make your call and pay afterwards. It is possible to make international calls from public telephones. Phonecards *(tarjeta telefónica)* for €6 or €12 can be purchased at kiosks, post offices and tobacconists. Reduced tariffs for international calls apply from 10pm to 8am and all day Sunday.

If you are using a US credit phone card, dial the company's access number below, then 01, and then the country code. Sprint tel: 900 99 0013; AT&T tel: 900 99 0011; MCI/Worldphone tel: 900 99 0014.

TIME

Spain is one hour ahead of Greenwich Mean Time (GMT +1). Summertime (GMT + 2) lasts from late March until the last Sunday in September.

NEWSPAPERS

Newsagents in Maó and Ciutadella always keep a good supply of English newspapers. The Menorcans themselves read the Spanish dailies *El País* and *El Mundo* to complement the island papers, the *Diario Insular*, *Diario de Mallorca* or *Diario 16 Baleares*.

ELECTRICITY

The usual voltage in hotels and holiday apartments is 220AC. Older establishments sometimes have the old 125-volt plugs. Plugs are two-pin and a continental adaptor is essential for visitors from Britain.

MEDICAL ASSISTANCE

All major tourist centres have *centros medicos*, where minor problems can be dealt with promptly; they usually require immediate payment. Hotel receptionists will help organise medical care in case of illness, too.

In Maó, Ciutadella, the major towns along the C271 and Es Migjorn Gran, several general practitioners can be found, as well as dentists *(dentistas)* and pharmacists *(farmácias)*. Pharmacists are highly trained and can dispense many drugs that would be available only on prescription in England.

EMERGENCIES

General emergencies 112; medical emergencies, also 061; Municipal Police: 092; National Police 091; Guardia Civil: 062 (traffic accidents outside cities, etc.); fire brigade *(bomberos)*: tel: 971 36 39 61 (Maó), and tel: 971 38 08 09 (Ciutadella).

Balearides (the name given to the islanders because of their throwing ability – *ballein* is the Greek word for throw). The sling was a vital weapon the islanders employed against foreign foes, and the slingsmen of Menorca were recruited as mercenaries, constituting an important division in Hannibal's armies as well as in the Roman force that conquered Carthage in 143BC.

ROMANS, CHRISTIANS AND MOORS

Under Quintus Caecilius Metellus, the Romans finally conquered the islands in 123BC. They fortified the local strongholds, constructed villas, baths and temples, and of course built their roads, such as the one that can still be seen on Puig de Santa Agueda *(see page 59)*. After the collapse of the Roman Empire, the Balearics were subjected to continuous plundering, and it was only after 1025 that a new cultural heyday emerged under the Moors. However, not many Arab buildings survived the Christian conquest at the beginning of the 13th century; most of them were either destroyed or incorporated into new structures. Ciutadella's main mosque, for example, became the Gothic cathedral. The Gothic pointed arch replaced the horseshoe arch of the Moors, but the Spanish did adopt the Moorish idea of arcaded courtyards and fountains, where water allowed.

> **Mystery of the *taules***
> How the incredibly heavy stones of the *taules* were placed on top of each other and connected without any technological assistance remains a mystery to this day, as does their significance. Did they represent deities, or were they used to mark cult sites?

Església del Roser in Ciutadella

In the Middle Ages, most building activity was of a religious nature, but later on magnificent secular buildings were constructed by merchants, landowners and wealthy artisans. Townhouses and *palazzi* were built in Ciutadella. With their richly decorated façades and beautiful courtyards, these buildings represented a fusion of the many different styles that came together in the Balearics, and some of them can still be admired today.

MENORCA'S FARMHOUSES

Crossing Menorca, you can't fail to notice all the white-washed farmhouses. Some might dominate a hilltop while others occupy a more modest position, stooped low against the ground as if cowering against the elements – braced for an onslaught of the north wind, the *tramuntana*. But whatever their location, these farmhouses all share a distinctive Menorcan style of architecture.

The central yards of these *llocs* are invariably surrounded by several buildings, which is why the locals refer to them in the plural, as *ses cases* – the houses. The northern side is usually occupied by outbuildings such as stables and dairies, which help protect the rest of the farm from the elements. Living quarters always face south, as does the patio area, which is usually furnished with a well, an oven for baking, a water trough and a round threshing floor made of brick. The entire complex is surrounded by a dry-stone wall.

Also typical is the protruding triple-arched porch area *(sa porxada)*; in the summer this is the focus of family life and in winter the venue for traditional livestock slaughtering and festivities *(matanzas)*. The roof of this porch doubles as a terrace. The shallow gable roof is in the typical Spanish style with terracotta tiles; terracotta pipes carry the water to underground storage cisterns.

The *llocs* are built of large limestone slabs *(marés)* obtained from the island's quarries. As the limestone is porous and lacks water resistance, the walls are treated with a coat of whitewash once a year, adding flashes of brightness to Menorca's already broad spectrum of colours.

Below: Ciutadella townhouses

Festivals

Steeped in centuries of tradition, Menorca's festivals are spectacular events, including fireworks, horse dancing and processions.

January 17: Fests d'es Tres Tocs, or festival of the three blows, held in Ciutadella to commemorate the *Reconquista* of Menorca in 1287.

March/April: Semana Santa, or Easter Week, at its most impressive in Maó and Ciutadella: religious celebrations and processions.

June 23 and 24: Festes de Sant Joan, the festival of St John, held in Ciutadella. Two days of equestrian fun, including the *jaleo (*horses' dance) on the Plaça d'es Born, which is crowned by a magnificent fireworks display. This is Menorca's most lively festival *(see also page 37)*.

July: On the **15th and 16th** boat processions in Maó, Ciutadella and Fornells. In the island's harbours the **Virgen del Carmen**, the patron saint of mariners and fishermen, is celebrated in colourful processions. On the third weekend in July is the **Festa de Sant Martí,** or festival of St Martin, with horseback processions and tournaments plus the traditional *jaleo*. On the fourth weekend is the **Festa de Sant Antoní** in Antonells in honour of the patron saint. The processions are crowned by a magnificent *jaleo* at the harbour.

August: A whole series of local **patron saint celebrations**, featuring processions and, especially, markets. The first weekend has celebrations in Es Migjorn Gran, the second in Alaior, the third in Sant Climent and the fourth in Sant Lluís, while Ferreries celebrates its saint on August 24 and 25.

September: 7th to 9th, Festes de la Vierge de Gracia, the festival of the Holy Virgin of Monte Toro, held in Maó; processions and a horseback parade with around 100 horses, all crowned by the biggest fireworks display on the island.

Below: jaleo in Ciutadella
Bottom: Festes de Gracia figure
Overleaf: local restaurant sign

FOOD AND DRINK

Menorca has a vast amount of delicious culinary delights. The overladen market stalls in the Claustre del Carme in Maó or at the Mercat in Ciutadella all prompt you to visit the nearest gourmet restaurant, especially in Es Mercadal or Es Migjorn Gran. Many meals begin with fresh bread and a small bowl of *alioli*, mayonnaise in its original form *(see overleaf)*. This overture is followed by the revelations of a hearty, filling and calorie-rich cuisine – as long as you stay away from any establishments boasting 'international cooking', which usually means there will be pizza, chips and hamburgers on the menu.

SEAFOOD ASSORTMENT

Top of the popularity list are the seafood dishes, especially *caldereta de langosta*, which is especially good in the restaurants of Fornells. A thick soup is prepared over high heat using tomatoes, onions, garlic, parsley, leek, a little cognac, and thinly sliced lobster, then poured onto slices of bread and served. Each cook refines the dish differently according to a personal recipe that is naturally kept secret. The only disadvantage of this superb dish is its price – you won't get one for less than around €28.

The *caldereta* family also includes two cheaper dishes, however: *caldereta de mariscos*, a shellfish soup, and *caldereta de pescado*, which contains several different kinds of fish. Lovers of fish will also be pleased to find pike, swordfish and perch on the menus here. A typically Menorcan variant is to bake the fish in the oven with potatoes and halved tomatoes.

Anyone who is eager to try a number of different kinds of fish should sample a *parillada de pescado*, which is varied and delicious. The island's cooks are just as good at shellfish and crustaceans: squid, mussels and seasnails are all expertly prepared.

Paella, the most popular tourist dish, can contain both fish *(paella marinera)* and meat. However, the classic ones usually feature saffron rice, chicken, pork, mussels, shrimps, cuttlefish, beans and peas.

FURTHER SPECIALITIES

Like their colleagues on the mainland, Menorcan cooks use a lot of onions, garlic and olive oil, but these are

Mahón Cheese

If the souvenir shops had anything to do with it, every visitor to Menorca would take home at least one *Queso de Mahón*. Regardless of the aroma and oppressive summer heat, no souvenir shop would be complete without a row of these colourfully packed cheeses.

Some of Menorca's cheese is still made by small family businesses, but most is now produced on a large scale. Since 1985, it has all carried the official label *Queso de Mahón*, although Alaior is the centre of production. Despite mechanisation, the cheese is still made in the traditional manner, except that cow's milk rather than sheep's milk is used. First, the whey is separated from the set milk using muslin. The cheese is then soaked for a day in salt water and left on a rack for a month where it is turned. A mix of butter, olive oil and paprika is then applied to the surface, and 2 months later the cheese is ready. According to maturity, the taste varies from tangy to spicy and the colour from deep yellow to ivory. After 8 months it has a similar texture to parmesan.

Queso de Mahón is best bought either straight from the farm or from a factory outlet in Alaior. You won't get the colourful packaging but you may get a glimpse of the cellars, and the price is lower than in souvenir shops.

enhanced by local ingredients such as cream, butter and *Queso de Mahón* (*see previous page*). Ingredients common to many meat dishes include capers, figs, cabbage, beans and artichokes. The meat ranges from pork and beef to rabbit, quail and partridge.

Whether it's *conejo con higos* (rabbit with dried figs) or *cordero con cebollas y alcaparras* (lamb with onions and capers), these oven-baked dishes are among the true highlights of Menorcan cuisine – especially if you happen to order them from the Ca n'Aguedet restaurant in Es Mercadal or El Gallo near Ferreries.

Special island delicacies include stuffed aubergines, peppers, courgettes and artichokes as well as the numerous simple soups enjoyed by the rural population, available in every pub: *oliaigua*, a vegetable soup consisting of tomatoes, onions, cabbage and toasted bread comes in all kinds of variations. The vegetable stew known as *tumbet*, baked with a cheese topping, contains sections of fried aubergine and potato.

Tapas, the famous Spanish appetisers, can be found in all variations on Menorca. Portions of fried squid , *albóndigas* (meat balls), spicy *chorizo*, and *butifarrone*, white or black sausages, are among the most famous. Tapas are often accompanied by *pa amb tomàquet*, bread rubbed with oil, garlic and tomato. Good snacks, which are also eaten as desserts, include *amargos* (almond-flavoured biscuits) and *ensaimadas* (yeast cakes fried in lard and topped with icing sugar), which are popular for breakfast.

THE SECRET OF MAYONNAISE

Menorcan still-lifes very often contain certain ingredients: eggs, half a lemon, a small bottle of olive oil, several cloves of garlic and a little salt. There is a special reason for this: the thick sauce known as *alioli*, served tepid, consists of these ingredients and was invented on Menorca. In 1756 the French had just driven the British (temporarily) from the island, and their leader, the Duke of Richelieu, wanted to celebrate the occasion.

A local cook created the exquisite sauce, the French adored it, took the recipe to Paris and left out the garlic, which may have contributed greatly to the global triumph of *salsa mahonesa*, better known as mayonnaise.

In another version of the story, the cook was a mistress of Richelieu's. In memory of his amorous escapade, he is reputed to have named this culinary speciality after the place where he met the *mahonesa* he had loved.

DRINKS

If you need something to settle your stomach after all this indulgence, try the *hierbas* – herbal liqueur that tastes of camomile – or *calent*, an aniseed, cinnamon and saffron liqueur that is drunk warm. The *palo* – a bitter-tasting brew made of gentian extract and various oriental herbs – is regarded as a stimulant. For something really refreshing, there is the local-brand *Xoriguer* gin, served in a 1:3 mixture with lemonade that is called a *pomada*.

Restaurant selection

The following restaurants on Menorca have been subdivided into three categories: €€€ = expensive, €€ = moderately priced, € = inexpensive.

Alaior

The Cobblers, Carrer de San Macario 6, tel: 971 37 14 00. An English-run restaurant in a converted cobbler's shop, with good chicken dishes and excellent salads. €€

Ximenes, Carrer Dr Albinana 2, tel: 971 37 11 20. This is a simple, smoky basement pub which serves delicious food that is both filling and cheap. **€**

Arenal d'en Castell
La Paella, Plaza de Mar 1, tel: 971 35 80 65. Right above the beach, with a terrace; lots of fish and meat dishes, liberally spiced with garlic. **€€€**

Biniancolla
Biniancolla, tel: 908 099061. Large restaurant terrace above the bay, great for dining at sunset, lots of seafood specialities, and great *paella*. **€€**

Binibeca Vell
El Pescadito, tel: 971 18 85 43. Pleasant place with vaulted ceiling, and large selection of fresh fish. **€€**
Bini Grill, tel: 971 15 05 94. Rustic restaurant with enormous Serrano hams hanging from the ceiling, and a shady inner courtyard. **€€**

Cala Marina
Cala Marina, Cala Molí 2, tel: 908-63 82 99. Beautiful restaurant above the bay with a roof terrace, numerous fish dishes, and massive *paellas*. **€€**

Cala Santa Galdana
La Cala, tel: 971 37 32 47. Has a viewing terrace, great seafood, and free *tapas* if you order a drink. **€€**
Es Barranc, Cala Santa Galdana, tel: 971 15 46 43. Right at the entrance to the Barranc d'Algendar, and the food is good despite the uninspired furnishings; try the fish balls. **€€**
El Mirador, tel: 908-79 98 47, uninspiring mass fare, but the location on a promontory off the bay is utterly superb. **€**

Cala Santandría
Sa Nacra, Cala Sa Caleta, tel: 971 38 62 06. Cave restaurant with Spanish cuisine on the next bay to the north of Cala Santandría. **€€**

Ciutadella
El Bribón, Marina 115, tel: 971 38 50 50. One of the most famous restaurants in the harbour, mainly does fish dishes. **€€**
Casa Manolo, Marina 117, tel: 971 38 00 03. Another popular seafood restaurant in the harbour, with air-conditioning, terrace and magnificent views. **€€**
Ca's Quintu, Plaça de Alfons III 4, tel: 971 38 10 02. A sunny restaurant with view of an old mill; the *boquerones en vinagre* (fresh anchovies in vinegar) are particularly good. **€**
Café Balear, Port de Ciutadella, tel: 971 38 00 05. Offers a good, reasonably priced set menu. **€€**

Es Mercadal
Ca n'Aguedet, Carrer Lepanto 23 and 30, tel: 971 37 53 91. Excellent rabbit, lamb and suckling pig dishes. The owners, the Vadell family, also produce the only wine on the island. **€€**
Ca n'Olga, Pont de na Macarrana, tel: 971 37 54 59. Hidden away behind an arch near the Torrente, with large garden terrace and stylish furnishings; very good Menorcan food, especially the seafood, quail and rabbit. **€€**
Molis d'es Reco, Carrer Vicario Fuxà

> **Water and wine**
> The water on Menorca is perfectly safe to drink but it has a rather distinctive taste. Most people drink bottled water – *agua mineral*. If you want it sparkling, ask for *agua con gas*, while still water is *agua sin gas*. *Fresca* means chilled, *natural* means straight off the shelf. Wine is usually drunk with meals, but as there is only one local producer – the Vadell family who own the Can'Aguedet *(see above)*, it nearly all comes from mainland Spain. Beer, both bottled and draught, is more popular with younger people.

5., tel: 971 37 53 92, old mill restaurant with a large terrace on the C721 that specialises in catering to large coach parties. **€**

Es Migjorn Gran

Migjorn, Carrer Major, tel: 971 37 01 1.. House with small courtyard terrace and select Menorcan dishes, all refined in an interesting way. **€**

S'Engolidor, Carrer Major 3, tel: 971 37 01 93. Great Menorcan dishes and a view over the gorge. Reservations essential. **€€**

Ferreries

El Gallo, Cta. Cala Santa Galdana, tel: 971 37 30 39. Old farmhouse restaurant serving good grilled meat. **€€**

Liorna, Carrer de Dalt 9, tel: 971 37 38 89. A nice little pizzeria, which also hosts interesting art exhibitions. **€€**

Fornells

Es Cranc, Carrer Escorles 31, tel: 971 37 64 42. Large, light establishment with excellent fish and a cheap lunchtime set menu. **€€**

El Pescador, Plaça s'Algaret 3, tel: 971 37 65 38. There are ceramic plates with crustacean motifs on the walls, and a huge fish menu, as well as a pleasant terrace and promenade. **€€**

Es Pla, Pasaje des Plá, tel: 971 37 66 55. Tastefully decorated seafood restaurant right beside the lagoon. Apparently King Juan Carlos sampled a *caldereta* here once. **€€**

Maó

Club Maritimo, Moll de Llevant 27, tel: 971 36 42 26. Elegant harbour-side restaurant serving delicious seafood, cooked to local, often experimental, recipes. Has a large terrace. **€€€**

Alba, Moll de Llevant 298, tel: 971 35 06 06. Good island cooking and attractive views. **€€**

Ca Na Pilar, Carrer Cardona y Orfila 61, tel: 971 36 68 17. Traditionl dishes of high quality; fish plus lamb and chicken. **€€**

Casa del Mar, Moll de Ponent 112, tel: 971 35 07 42. Delicious fish, large helpings, too. **€**

Il Porto, Moll de Llevant 225, tel: 971 35 44 26. Busy place, with a huge menu. **€**

La Tropical, Luna 36, tel: 971 36 05 56. Island dishes at a price that won't hurt your budget. **€**

Roma, Moll de Llevant 295, tel: 971 35 37 77. Most popular pizzeria in Maó, and the pizzas are absolutely enormous. **€**

San Tomás

Es Bruc, Carretera San Adeoato, tel: 971 37 04 88. Meals served on a large terrace above the beach; good selection of *tapas*. **€**

Sant Climent

Casino Sant Climent, Carrer de Sant Jaume 4, tel: 971 15 34 18. Simple food, served to the accompaniment of good jazz on Tuesday and Thursday, when musicians are welcome to bring their own instruments and join in. **€**

Sant Lluís

Pan y Vino, Torret 52, tel: 971 15 03 22. This is *the* place for Menorcan cuisine and select wines. Set in the village of Torret, near Sant Lluís, it is elegant, intimate, and very popular with the local expatriate population. **€€€**

El Picadero, Cta Maó–San Lluis, tel: 971 36 32 68. British-run restaurant with a barbecue and lots of meat. **€€**

La Venta, Carrer de Sant Lluís, tel: 971 15 09 95. Rustically furnished restaurant/bar with traditional Menorcan cuisine. **€€**

La Rueda, Carrer de Sant Lluís 30, tel: 971 15 11 84. A friendly bar with dishes typical of the island and a varied selection of *tapas*. **€**

ACTIVE HOLIDAYS

BEACHES

Despite some wonderful hiking routes and the 9-hole golf course of Son Bou, the sea is naturally the focal point of tourist interest on Menorca.

The island has bays and beaches to suit every taste, and they really are picturesque. There are huge differences, however: on the Platja de Son Bou or the Cala Santa Galdana with their high-rise hotels, be prepared to share the beach with many others. Things are far quieter on the beaches known as *platjes verges* to the southeast of Ciutadella. Not all the beaches can be easily reached by car, and the last section often has to be done on foot. Bays like Cala en Turqueta, Cala des Talaier or Son Saura are worth walking to, in any case. Topless sunbathing is a common sight now (but do cover up when you leave the beach); nudism is still only possible in the most remote bays such as Cala Macarellata.

HIKING

Menorca is ideal for short or long hikes, and it's easy to orient yourself according to landmarks like Monte Toro or the Puig de Santa Àgueda. The best starting points for hikes are Ferreries, Alaior, Fornells and Es Mercadal. A word of warning, however: many of the routes are not properly marked, and even expensive maps leave a lot to be desired. The best maps are those from the Servicio Geográfico del Ejército, on scales of 1:50 000 and 1:25 000 respectively. You can get them in bookshops in Maó and Ciutadella if you show your passport.

The Camí de Cavalls *(see page 11)*, is also marked on these maps: in the north and southwest it leads through remote regions of great natural beauty. If you are crossing private property, be sure to close all gates and fences behind you so that farmers don't get annoyed.

For information on guided walks, contact the Oficina d'Informació Turística in Maó and Ciutadella *(see page 113)*. Bird-watching trips and other nature tours are organised by the GOB (Carrer d'Isabel II, 42, Maó, tel: 971 35 07 63).

CYCLING

Bikes can be hired from several shops in Ciutadella, Maó and most of the holiday centres. They cost around €4

*Surfing and swiming
at Cala en Porter*

a day to hire. Mountain bikes are a better bet than touring bikes because quite a few roads and beach-access tracks are incredibly bumpy. You don't need to be particularly athletic or good at climbing gradients, however.

The old Camí d'en Kane *(see page 50)* and the Camí de Binifabini near Alaior in the north are easy and quiet.

RIDING

On Menorca, horses are either bred for racing or used as work animals; riding is purely for visitors. The meetings at racecourses in Maó and Ciutadella are well attended every week, because Menorcans are happier to bet on horses than to ride them. Day-long riding trips are available from around 20 stables, including the Rancho Allenwood (tel: 971 15 30 71) near Sant Climent and Club Hipic es Boeret (tel: 971 15 10 49 at S'Algar. The Hort de Llucaitx Park (Carretera Maó–Fornells, km 17, tel 629 39 28 94), also has horses and ponies for hire.

WATERSPORTS

Menorca is ideal for windsurfers and sailors, whether beginners, keen amateurs or professionals. The holiday centres and marinas in the south of the island are the best places to head for. Punta Prima and the nearby Cala en Bosc are both very good for windsurfing. Fornells has a yacht club that offers surfing courses and rents out equipment, and it is perfectly located on a long bay. The club also has a sailing school and 50 berths.

The larger towns are also popular with watersports enthusiasts: the Club Náutico de Ciutadella (tel: 971 38 11 46) for instance, runs sailing courses lasting several weeks. The Club Marítimo de Maó (tel: 971 36 50 22) is also a good sailing school. The most ambitious of all of them is the Club S'Algar Diving and Watersports (tel: 971 15

06 01) in Cala d'Alcaufar, where you can learn anything from windsurfing to water-skiing with a paraglider. Lengthy diving sessions along the reefs and in the grottos of the rocky south coast; many are only accessible from underwater. The Diving Centre, Cala Torret, tel: 971 18 85 28 offers introductions to scuba as well as daily diving trips. Scuba Menorca (tel: 971 35 13 63) in Maó, is a recommended diving school. So is Diving Center Fornells, Passeig Marítim 44B, Fornells, tel: 971 376 431 in the north.

Nightlife

Nightlife roughly falls into two categories: the loud late-night action in the bigger resorts, where you will rub shoulders almost exclusively with other tourists; and the more indigenous spots, mostly in Maó and Ciutadella. The island's discos come and go in the popularity stakes (and are only open in summer). The old warehouse area behind the marina in Ciutadella throbs with noisy venues. Things don't get moving until late: some places don't open until 11pm but once open, they keep going.

A few bars and clubs that have stood the test of time are:

Akelaare, Moll de Ponent 42, Maó, tel: 971 36 85 20. Music and cocktails in an upmarket bar on the harbour.

Asere, Carrer Corniola 23, Ciutadella, tel 971 38 38 52. A salsa club where nothing happens until very late.

Casino Sant Climent, Carrer de Sant Jaume 4, tel: 971 15 34 18. Good jazz sessions on Tuesday and Thursday; musicians are welcome to bring their own instruments and join in.

El Salón, Carrer Victor 28, Es Castell. Satire, song, dance and excellent theatre by a small troupe, including female impersonaters.

Piano Bar, Carrer Sant Ignasi, Es Castell, tel: 971 36 40 22. As laid-back as it sounds.

ACCOMMODATION

You must book well in advance if you want to find any accommodation whatsoever on Menorca during the peak season. To maintain its green image, the island has increased the standard of its tourism: higher quality facilities have replaced those geared to mass tourism, and building restrictions are in force everywhere.

Menorca has to provide accommodation for an increasing number of visitors. Even though 40,000 beds are available in hotels and apartments, private holiday homes provide far more accommodation – after all, up to 800,000 visitors have to be catered for annually, and the majority of them arrive between May and September.

ENDLESS VARIETY
Accommodation on offer ranges from luxury hotels to private holiday homes, modern club villages and simple boarding houses. Categories and stars are not usually a reliable guide to the quality – the ugly concrete highrise hotels at Son Bou, for instance, all products of the construction boom in the 1970s, are high-category establishments, because of the facilities they offer, while one-star hotels like the Del Almirante in Es Castell or the boarding house S'Engolidor in Es Migjorn Gran with its nostalgic charm and family-run atmosphere can be far more pleasant places to stay.

VILLAS AND HOLIDAY HOMES
The best type of holiday accommodation for families on Menorca is that provided by the innumerable private villas and holiday homes, most of them British-owned and rented out via travel agencies. You can expect two to three bedrooms, a kitchen, a comfortable living room, a terrace and usually a swimming pool too. The houses are almost all in residential areas beside the sea, but whatever the brochures might promise, don't expect them to be in remote locations. A tiny piece of lawn and a few palm trees do provide some privacy, however, and are sufficient for most self-catering visitors.

HOTELS AND APARTMENTS
The above comments about holiday homes also apply to the numerous apartments on the island, which are usually attached to hotels – so all the

Chatting in Ciutadella

usual hotel amenities can be enjoyed, but you also have the privacy of your own rooms. The club villages close to the coasts like S'Algar or Son Parc provide similar amenities, combining sports, excursions and accommodation. Hotels on Menorca also offer numerous opportunities to combine fitness and fun, with tennis courts, boat and surfboard hire, and the instructors to go with them, if desired. Most hotels are along the south coast, and are marketed by package tour operators.

Ciutadella and Maó provide the largest variety of accommodation possibilities, from simple youth hostels to first-class hotels; in the centre of the island there's a lot less choice. In towns like Es Migjorn Gran, Es Mercada or Ferreries, for instance, there are only one or two *hostales* available. They tend to be far away from the tourist centres, with clean, simple rooms, moderate prices and restaurants attached.

> **Rural alternative**
> An alternative is offered by Agroturismo – accommodation in a range of country houses. Information from tourist offices in Maó and Ciutadella (*see page 113*), or Asociación Agroturisme Balear, Av. Gabriel Alama 8a, Palma, tel: 971 72 15 08.

CAMPING

There is a campsite, **S'Atalaia**, tel: 971 37 30 95, on the road from Ferreries to Cala Santa Galdana, and another, **Son Bou**, tel: 971 37 26 05, on the Platja de Son Bou.

Hotel selection

The following hotels have been subdivided into three categories: **€€€** = expensive, **€€** = moderately priced, **€** = inexpensive.

Biniancolla
Sur Menorca, tel: 971 15 18 00. Cheap hotel near the sea, popular with package tourists. **€**

Cala Blanca
Cala Blanca, tel: 971 38 04 50. Large hotel surrounded by palms and pines, with swimming pool. **€€€**
Mediterrani, Urbanización Cala Blanca, tel: 971 38 42 03. Modern and comfortable; near the beach. **€€**
Sagitario Playa, Avinguda de la Platja 4, tel: 971 38 28 77. Friendly; has its own tennis courts. **€€**

Cala d'Alcaufar
S'Algar, Urbanización S'Algar, tel: 971 15 17 00. Luxury hotel right by the sea with restaurant, bar and pool. **€€€**
Xuroy, Cala d'Alcaufar, tel: 971 15 18 20. A recently renovated and attractive establishment with a large beach terrace, and sea views from balconies on 1st and 2nd floors; surfboards and diving equipment can be hired inhouse. **€€**

Cala en Bosc
Cala en Bosc, Cala en Bosc, tel: 971 38 06 00. Close to the marina, this large hotel has its own windsurfing school. **€€€**
Club Falcó, Son Xoriguer, tel: 971 38 46 23. An attractive holiday village with an extensive park, plus lots of sporting facilities. **€€**

Cala en Forcat
Almirante Farragut, Cala en Forcat, tel: 971 38 80 00. Good service and comfortable rooms, many with sea views, in this hotel which sits above the long bay. **€€**

Cala en Porter
Playa Azul, Passeig Marítim, tel: 971 37 74 21. Right on the beach, and with a swimming pool as well. **€€**

Cala Santa Galdana

Audax, tel: 971 37 31 25. Square, 1960s-style building designed for package tourists, right beside sea. €€
Cala Galdana, tel: 971 15 45 00. This hotel also has an apartment-bungalow community for families. €€
Sol Gavilanes, tel: 971 15 45 45. Comfortable and enormous hotel in a park above the beach; restaurant terrace has a sea view. €€

Cala Santandría

Poseidon, tel: 971 38 26 44. Small and comfortable establishment with family atmosphere, right by the beach. €€
Ses Voltes, tel: 971 38 04 00. Also on the beach; larger than the above. €€

Ciutadella

Patricia, Passeig San Nicolau 90–92, tel: 971 38 55 11, fax: 971 48 11 20. Modern, well-appointed hotel in a quiet position overlooking the port a few minutes' from Plaça del Born. Small pool. €€
Esmeralda, Passeig Sant Nicolau 171, tel: 971 38 02 50; fax: 971 48 11 20. A comfortable establishment with a view of the harbour entrance; there's a pool and a tennis court. €€
Playa Grande, Carrer Obispo Juano 2, tel: 971 36 43 62. Modern hotel with good restaurant, just 10 minutes' walk from the centre. €€
Ciutadella, Carrer Sant Eloi 10, tel: 971 38 34 62. Simple hotel near the Plaça Alfons III; most rooms with bath; a restaurant with good Menorcan cuisine. €
Hostal Madrid, Carrer Madrid 60, tel: 971 38 03 28. Restaurant pool and pleasant garden. Not far from the town centre. €
Oasis, Carrer Sant Isidre 33, tel: 971 38 21 97. In a peaceful park with a fountain and trees but also close to the centre. Has a bar and café and terrace. Good value for the moderate price. €

Es Mercadal

Hostal Jeni, Miranda del Toro 81, tel: 971 37 50 59, fax: 971 37 51 24. This *hostal* offers simple but clean rooms in the town centre. There's a swimming pool in the garden, and a good restaurant. €

Es Migjorn Gran

S'Engolidor, Carrer Major 3, tel: 971 37 01 93. Stylish establishment with terrace above a *barranc*, easy to miss because it's not signposted. There is naive art on the walls and good-value Menorcan cuisine, plus four simple guest rooms. €

Ferreries

Loar, Reverendo Padre Huguet 2, tel: 971 37 41 81. Modern apartment hotel in the town centre; 30 rooms. €€
Binisaid, 5km (3 miles) to the south, on the right-hand side of the road from Ferreries to Cala Santa Galdana, tel: 971 36 22 99. 'Farmhouse holiday'-style family apartments with kitchen and bathroom. €
La Perdiz, Carrer Maó 14, tel: 971 37 30 48. Simple hostel in the new section of Ferreries. €

Fornells

Hostal Fornells, Carrer Major 17, tel: 971 37 66 76; fax: 971 37 66 88 Advertises itself as a 'health eco resort' with lots of sports activities (biking, diving, windsurfing, sailing, water skiing, golf, exercise and nutrition programmes). Small pool. €€
La Palma, Plaça S'Algaret 3, tel: 971 37 64 87; fax: 971 37 66 34. Right by the harbour, a friendly place with simply-furnished rooms, some overlooking the sea, others the garden and pool. Busy local bar on ground floor. €
Residencia Port Fornells, Ses Salines, tel: 971 37 63 73. Popular with sailors and windsurfers; south of the town on the lagoon. €€

Tramontana Park, Platjes de Fornells, tel: 971 37 67 42. An agreeable apartment hotel with one-, two- and three-room apartments, a restaurant and pool. **€€**

S'Algaret, Plaça S'Algaret 7, tel: 971 37 66 74. Basic accommodation, but clean and central. **€**

Maó

Port Maó, Avingunda Fort de l'Eau 13, tel: 971 36 26 00. Very comfortable rooms in a colonial-style building. Swimming pool and attractive gardens. **€€€**

Capri, Carrer Sant Esteve 8, tel: 971 36 14 00. Modern hotel to the west of the town. **€€**

Sol Mirador des Port, Carrer Dalt Vilanova 1, tel: 971 36 00 16. A pleasant place with (as the name suggests) a view of the harbour. Swimming pool. **€€**

Miramar, Puerto de Maó 44, tel: 971 36 29 00; fax: 971 35 12 40. West of the city, good value; child care is available if required. **€€**

Orsi, Carrer Infanta 19, tel: 971 36 47 51. Simple ,British-run hostel on the edge of the centre; ask for the room with a roof terrace because the views are fantastic. **€**

Platja d'en Castell

Castell Playa, Platja d'en Castell, tel: 971 35 80 88. A beachside hotel, with love y views. **€€**

Club Hotel Aquamarina, Platja d'en Castell, tel: 971 35 80 60. Next to the Castell Playa, this is one of the biggest hotels in Arenal d'en Castell. Rooms have sea views, and there is a sauna; good place for families. **€€**

Punta Prima

Xaloc, tel: 971 15 01 06. Pleasant hotel near the beach with big pool and mini-golf range. Inner courtyard plus restaurant shaded by pines. **€€**

Pueblo Menorca, tel: 971 15 18 50. With 538 rooms this is by far the largest hotel on Menorca, and everything is geared towards mass tourism – so it's cheap but often fully booked by tour operators in high season. **€**

Punta Prima, tel: 971 15 07 14. Simple single or double rooms. **€**

Sant Lluís

Biniali, Carrer Sestra-Sant Lluís 50, tel: 971 15 17 24. Restored *finca* southwest of town; quiet, elegant, with pool and large terrace; book early. **€€€**

Sant Tomás

Sant Tomás, Platja de Sant Tomás, tel: 971 37 00 25. Luxury, medium-sized hotel right beside the beach. **€€€**

Lord Nelson, Urbanización Sant Tomás, tel: 971 37 01 25. Near the beach; two swimming pools. **€€**

Victoria Playa, Platja Sant Tomás, tel: 971 37 02 00. On the beach, with a pool and children's play area. **€€**

Son Bou

Las Marismas, Urbanización Torre Solí, tel: 971 37 80 40. Luxurious 'aparthotel'. **€€€**

Son Valentín Menorca, Urbanización Torre Solí, tel: 971 37 27 48. Pleasant 'aparthotel' attractively set in

---

Visitors with disabilities

Menorca is not perhaps the best place for people with reduced mobility, but things are gradually improving.

Among the hotels that have wheelchair access are the Aquamarina in Platja d'en Castell, the Cala Blanca and Sagitario Playa, in Cala Blanca, the Victoria Playa in Sant Tomás and the Son Valentín Menorca apartment-hotel in Son Bou, which has some user-friendly rooms (see the alphabetical listings for full details of these establishments).

✻ INSIGHT COMPACT GUIDES

Great Little Guides to the following destinations:

Algarve	Goa	St Petersburg	North York Moors
Amsterdam	Gran Canaria	Salzburg	Northumbria
Athens	Greece	Shanghai	Oxford
Bahamas	Holland	Singapore	Peak District
Bali	Hong Kong	Southern Spain	Scotland
Bangkok	Ibiza	Sri Lanka	Scottish
Barbados	Iceland	Switzerland	Highlands
Barcelona	Ireland	Sydney	Shakespeare
Beijing	Israel	Tenerife	Country
Belgium	Italian Lakes	Thailand	Snowdonia
Berlin	Italian Riviera	Toronto	South Downs
Bermuda	Jamaica	Turkey	York
Brittany	Jerusalem	Turkish Coast	Yorkshire Dales
Bruges	Kenya	Tuscany	
Brussels	Laos	Venice	*USA regional*
Budapest	Lisbon	Vienna	*titles:*
Burgundy	Madeira	Vietnam	Boston
California	Madrid	West of Ireland	Cape Cod
Cambodia	Mallorca		Chicago
Chile	Malta	*UK regional*	Florida
Copenhagen	Menorca	*titles:*	Florida Keys
Costa Brava	Milan	Bath &	Hawaii – Maui
Costa del Sol	Montreal	Surroundings	Hawaii – Oahu
Costa Rica	Morocco	Belfast	Las Vegas
Crete	Moscow	Cambridge &	Los Angeles
Cuba	Munich	East Anglia	Martha's Vineyard
Cyprus	Normandy	Cornwall	& Nantucket
Czech Republic	Norway	Cotswolds	Miami
Denmark	Paris	Devon & Exmoor	New Orleans
Dominican	Poland	Edinburgh	New York
Republic	Portugal	Glasgow	San Diego
Dublin	Prague	Guernsey	San Francisco
Egypt	Provence	Jersey	Washington DC
Finland	Rhodes	Lake District	
Florence	Rio de Janeiro	London	
French Riviera	Rome	New Forest	

Insight's checklist to meet all your travel needs:

- *Insight Guides* provide the complete picture, with expert cultural background and stunning photography. Great for travel planning, for use on the spot, and as a souvenir. 180 titles.
- *Insight Pocket Guides* focus on the best choices for places to see and things to do, picked by our correspondents. They include large fold-out maps. More than 120 titles.
- *Insight Compact Guides* are fact-packed books to carry with you for easy reference when you're on the move in a destination. More than 130 titles.
- *Insight Maps* combine clear, detailed cartography with essential information and a laminated finish that makes the maps durable and easy to fold. 125 titles.
- *Insight Phrasebooks* and *Insight Travel Dictionaries* are very portable and help you find exactly the right word in French, German, Italian and Spanish.

The world's largest collection of visual travel guides and maps

INDEX